THE
FINANCIAL SECTOR
OF THE AMERICAN
ECONOMY

edited by
STUART BRUCHEY
UNIVERSITY OF MAINE

A GARLAND SERIES

MEASURING RISKS OF DEPOSIT INSTITUTIONS

HG
1660
.U5
S65
1994
West

FRANK M. SONG

GARLAND PUBLISHING, Inc.
New York & London / 1994

Library of Congress Cataloging-in-Publication Data

Song, Frank M., 1962–
    Measuring risks of deposit institutions / Frank M. Song.
        p.   cm. — (The Financial sector of the American economy)
    Includes bibliographical references and index.
    ISBN 0–8153–1684–4 (alk. paper)
    1. Deposit banking—United States.   2. Risk—United States.
I. Title. II. Series.
HG1660.U5S65   1994
332.1'752—dc20   93–41569
                                                            CIP

Printed on acid-free, 250-year-life paper
Manufactured in the United States of America

To

My Family

Contents

Preface

One of the most challenging questions facing deposit-institution regulators and managers is to assess the risk exposures of the institution to a macroeconomic environment. This book takes the approach of market assessment of deposit institutions by examining the stock returns of a sample of deposit institutions in order to assess their riskiness. Risk exposures of deposit institutions to a macroeconomic environment, as proxied by changes in the stock market return, interest rate, inflation, and industrial production, are studied. In addition, I also develop statistical models to study the time-varying risks of deposit institutions and their relationship with the macroeconomic variables and asset compositions.

The book consists of three essays. Essay I (Chapter II) examines the macroeconomic risk exposure of the deposit institutions within the context of the Arbitrage Pricing Theory (APT). Previous studies focus exclusively on risk exposures to the market and interest rate factors, ignoring other potentially important factors. This essay asks whether three macroeconomic factors, in addition to the market and interest rates, are priced in the deposit-institution stock returns. The three factors considered are: 1) the change in industrial production, 2) the default risk premium, and 3) the unexpected inflation. I investigate a multi-factor model with these measured macroeconomic factors and then impose nonlinear cross-sectional restrictions implied by the APT. Nonlinear Seemingly Unrelated Regression (NLSUR) is used to obtain the joint estimates of factor sensitivities and their associated risk premiums. The major findings of this essay are that the total risk premium is dominated by both the market and interest rate factors and that only these two factors are priced. This result confirms the importance of interest rate risk and market risk in banking.

Essay II (Chapter III) builds on the findings of Essay I and specifies a two-factor model with the market and interest rate factors in a conditional environment. The market and interest rate risks are measured by their time-varying betas. These betas are ratios of the conditional covariance of the stock returns with the factor and the conditional variance of the factor. The time-varying risks are studied by applying the Autoregressive Conditional Heteroskedasticity (ARCH) modeling method. The resulting two-factor ARCH model is estimated by the generalized method of moments (GMM). The results suggest that the market risks were very volatile over the sample period 1977-87, and they became higher and more volatile after 1982. The interest rate risks were more stable, and they did not respond to the Fed's change in monetary policy in 1979 and 1982. Specification tests suggest the usefulness of my two-factor ARCH model in the study of deposit-institution stock returns.

Essay III (Chapter IV) examines the effect of macroeconomic variables and bank asset-composition variables on the risks of four portfolios of bank holding companies (BHC's) for the years, 1973-1990, using a much broader data set of bank stock returns and macroeconomic and financial variables. A two-step approach is developed. First, I apply a moving-regression technique to the two-index model with market and interest-rate indices. The results suggest that market beta changed substantially over the sample period. In contrast, the interest-rate beta is less significant. In the second step, I regress the moving market beta on a set of macroeconomic variables (money supply, industrial production, interest rates, and exchange rates) and a number of bank-asset composition variables and find that these macroeconomic variables and banks' real-estate exposure affect the market risks of the sample commercial banks significantly. The effects are also found to differ somewhat between the money-center banks and other banks.

I am indebted to numerous individuals for their comments on this book and for their encouragement. In particular, I owe deep gratitude to K.C. Chan, Paul Evans, Ed Kane, Nelson Mark, and James Thomson. I also thank my colleagues in the Department of Economics at Cleveland State University for providing a friendly and encouraging environment for me to revise, extend, and complete this project for publication. Special thanks to Therese Simon for her excellent typing job and for her assistance in organizing the manuscript of this book.

Illustrations

List of Figures

List of Tables

xv

Chapter I

Introduction

Assessing risks faced by deposit institutions is of greater concern for regulators because of the perceived link between the stability of the deposit-institution system and the performance of the economy. It is also a concern for deposit-institution managers to be able to measure and control the risks of deposit institutions. This study seeks to measure the risks of deposit institutions by examining the behavior of their stock returns. Macroeconomic risks of a sample of actively-traded deposit institutions are identified and the Autoregressive Conditional Heteroscedastic (ARCH) modeling method and a two-stage approach are used to study the time-variation of the risks for the time period of the 1970's and 1980's.

The reason for studying this time period is that, from the late 1970's to the 1980's, the economic environment facing deposit institutions changed greatly. In October, 1979, the Federal Reserve changed its policy target from controlling the level of the interest rate to controlling the quantity of the money supply. In October, 1982, the Fed switched back from stabilizing the monetary aggregates to stabilizing the level of interest rates. Interest rates were most volatile from October, 1979 to October, 1982. The Depository Institutions Deregulation and Monetary Control Act (DIDMCA) of 1980 and the Garn-St. Germain Act of 1982 marked other major steps toward greater competition for the deposit-institution industry.

The changing economic environment for the deposit-institution industry since the late 1970's poses a serious challenge to both regulators and managers. In order to protect their

1

insurance fund and ensure the proper risk-taking of deposit institutions, deposit-institution regulators are increasingly interested in risk-related deposit insurance and capital standard. However, to design risk-related deposit insurance and capital standard requires precise measurement of the risks of deposit institutions. Deposit-institution managers are also very interested in risk measurement because of the need for designing financial hedges against the increasing uncertainties facing deposit institutions.

One approach to assessing the risks of a deposit institution can be called the accounting assessment, which applies some accounting values of the balance sheet to measure the risks of deposit institutions. For example, maturity gap measures are intended to provide an assessment of interest rate risk. Details on loan portfolio data provide measures for potential credit risks. The accounting approach suffers from the following problems: (1) the assets and liabilities are calculated at their par values, not their market values, (2) the values of intangible assets and deposit-insurance guarantees are not shown in the accounting measures, and (3) the increasing popularity of off-balance sheet activities of deposit institutions are not adequately assessed. In addition, the accounting measures tend to look at the performance of the past, not the expected changes in the future.

Another approach to assessing the risks of a deposit institution can be called the market assessment, which examines the exposure of stock returns of deposit institutions to the uncertainties of macroeconomic variables in the economy. Stock returns of deposit institutions are believed to be effective in measuring the risks of the institutions. Since movements in stock returns depend upon expectations of future events, such as inflation, monetary policy, levels and volatilities of interest rates, and changes in Gross National Product (GNP), market information on stock returns of deposit institutions can provide a good measure of the exposure of these institutions to macroeconomic risks. To believers in the efficiency of financial markets, market assessment of risks of deposit institutions is the only sensible way since the deposit-institution stock returns reflect all relevant information about the risk exposure of a deposit institution. The information embedded in the stock returns summarizes all the pertinent facts about the deposit-institution balance sheet, the off-balance sheet, and intangible assets. The market measures have the forward-looking nature in the sense that market value reflects expected earnings of institutions.

The literature on the market assessment of risks of deposit institutions is sizeable and growing. Lynge and Zumwalt [1980], Chance and Lane [1980], Flannery and James [1984], Giliberto [1985], and Kane and Unal [1988] try to identify risks of deposit institutions by applying a two-index version of the market model. The two indexes used are a market index and an interest rate index. The coefficient on the market index, the so-called "market beta" or "market risk," is a measure of the riskiness of a given stock or portfolio relative to the risk inherent in the stock market as a whole. Some of the activities of a deposit institution, such as loan default and shifts in operating expenses, are likely to react to the same events that move the value of the market portfolio. The coefficient on the interest rate index, the so-called "interest rate beta" or "interest rate risk," measures the sensitivity of deposit-institution stock returns to a change in the interest rate. Interest rate risk occurs because of what is termed the "mismatch maturity," i.e., interest payments on the liability side do not always change in the same magnitude as interest receipts on the asset side of the deposit-institution balance sheet as the level of interest rate changes. Flannery and James [1984] show that common stock returns for a sample of actively-traded deposit institutions are correlated with a market index and interest rate changes. The interest rate sensitivity of a firm's common stocks is related to the maturity composition of the firm's nominal assets and liabilities. Rosenberg and Perry [1981] apply the Capital Asset Pricing Model (CAPM) to bank stock returns and suggest the existence of an "extramarket" component which differs both from market risk and residual risk. They argue that the "extramarket" factor can be thought of as an industry group factor which is intermediate between systematic market risk and specific risk. Sweeney and Warga [1986] study the two-factor model, with market and change in the yield on a long-term government bond as the factors, to show that the interest rate factor is priced in the sense of the Arbitrage Pricing Theory (APT). Looking at 21 industries, they suggest that only utility and bank stock returns are interest-rate sensitive. Kane and Unal [1988] investigate variability over the period 1975-1985 in the risk components of both bank and savings and loan stock. They use the Goldfeld and Quandt switching regression method to show that market beta, interest rate beta, and residual risk of deposit-institution stock vary significantly during this period. Both 1979 and 1982 are affirmed as years when there were regime changes of the return-generating process for deposit-institution stocks. The market beta and interest rate beta shift to different values as the deposit institutions go through different regimes.

This study, following the tradition of Lloyd and Shick [1974], Lynge and Zumwalt [1980], Chance and Lane [1980], Flannery and James [1984], Giliberto [1985], and Kane and Unal [1988], adopts the market assessment of risks of deposit institutions. There are three essays in this book.

Essay I, which is contained in Chapter II, studies the macroeconomic risk exposures of a sample of deposit institutions by examining the response of the deposit-institution stock returns to that of macroeconomic variables within the framework of the APT. Deposit institutions are exposed to a macroeconomic risk if the macroeconomic variable is priced in the sense of the APT. That is, the contribution associated with the macroeconomic variable to the total risk premium in the APT model is significant. This first essay improves upon previous studies in that it identifies macroeconomic risks other than market and interest rate risks. It investigates whether the unexpected changes in macroeconomic variables, like interest rates, inflation, industrial production, and default risk premia, affect the value of a sample of deposit institutions. It is found that all deposit-institution stocks in the sample are sensitive to both the interest rate factor and the residual market factor, but less than one-third of the deposit-institution stocks are sensitive to the default risk premia factor. The deposit-institution stocks are not sensitive to either the unexpected inflation factor or the industrial production factor. It is further found that, among the four macroeconomic variables, only interest rate risk is strongly priced in the sense of the APT, i.e., investors in deposit-institution stocks demand compensation for taking interest rate risk. The result confirms the importance of studying the two-factor model, with a market factor and an interest rate factor, in banking literature. The total risk premium, the risk premiums for the macroeconomic factors, and the residual market factor provide useful information for bank regulators to price deposit insurance. The interest rate factor consists of the largest share of the total risk premium.

Chapter II is divided into several sections. Section 2.1 surveys the theory and application of the APT. Section 2.2 gives the empirical specification of the APT as a Multivariate Nonlinear Regression model with some macroeconomic variables and presents the Iterated Nonlinear Seemingly Unrelated Regression (ITNSUR) estimation technique. Section 2.3 explains the sample deposit-institution stock returns and the four macroeconomic variables used in the APT model. The empirical results are reported in Section 2.4. Section 2.5 concludes Essay I.

The results of Essay I suggest that we can probably focus on the two-factor model, with the market and interest rate factors, in studying the issue of the macroeconomic risk exposure of deposit institutions. Essay II, which is contained in Chapter III, further seeks to explain the market risk and interest rate risk based on Merton's [1973] theory of the multi-factor asset pricing model. The two-factor model with market and interest rate factors is justified by Merton's Intertemporal Capital Asset Pricing Model (ICAPM). The market risk and interest rate risk are measured by the two betas in a two-factor model, with the market portfolio as one factor and an interest rate index as the other. Inspired by the work of Kane and Unal [1988], I assume that the expected returns and betas are not constant over the sample period chosen. However, instead of applying Goldfeld and Quandt's switching regression methods as in Kane and Unal [1988], I apply an Autoregressive Conditional Heteroscedastic (ARCH) model to study the time-varying market risk and interest rate risk. The specific ARCH model used is an extension of the model of Bodurtha and Mark [1987] and Mark [1988] to a two-factor case. The advantage of using the ARCH modeling strategy for the two-factor model is that it allows the conditional covariance (variance) as a function of past conditional covariance (variance) and identifies the dynamic changes of the market risk and interest rate risk of deposit institutions. This further extends the work of Kane and Unal [1988] to a continuous case.

The innovations of Essay II are twofold. First, the time-varying market risk and interest rate risk of a sample of deposit institutions are studied within the framework of a two-factor ARCH model. The two betas are specified as the ratios of a conditional covariance and a conditional variance which allows me to identify the time-varying risks. Second, to my knowledge, this is the first attempt to apply the ARCH modeling strategy to a two-factor model.

The results of Essay II suggest that the market risk and interest rate risk of my sample deposit institutions changed during the period 1977-1987. The market risks are higher and more volatile after 1982. The interest rate risks are less volatile than the market risks, and there is evidence of an increase in the interest risks since the end of 1982. Contrary to popular belief, the interest rate risks of the deposit institutions did not respond in any significant way to the regime change in the monetary policy of the Federal Reserve in 1979 and 1982. Model specification tests suggest the usefulness of the two-factor ARCH model in studying deposit-institution stock returns.

Chapter III is divided into six sections. Section 3.1 discusses the theory of the multi-factor asset pricing model. Section 3.2

examines the two-factor model--with the market and an interest rate index as the two factors--for deposit institutions in a conditional environment, and it also discusses the estimation method. Section 3.3 analyzes the sample data. Section 3.4 provides the empirical specification and estimation. Section 3.5 discusses the empirical results and compares them with those obtained in previous studies. Conclusions and further research plans are given in Section 3.6.

Chapter IV contains Essay III. In this chapter, a moving-regression approach is adapted to measure the changing risks of banks. The effect of macroeconomic variables and bank asset-composition variables on the risks of four portfolios of bank holding companies (BHC's) for the years 1973-1990 is examined. Based on the results of Chapter II, the focus is on a two-index model with market and interest rate factors. A two-step approach is developed. First, a moving-regression technique is applied to the two-index market model. The results suggest that the market beta changed substantially over the sample period, while the interest rate beta is less significant. In the second step, the moving market beta is regressed on a set of macroeconomic variables (money supply, industrial production, interest rates, and exchange rates) and a number of bank asset-composition variables, and it is found that these macroeconomic variables and bank real-estate-loan exposure both affect the market risk of the sample commercial banks significantly. The effects are also found to differ somewhat between the money-center banks and other banks.

The organization of the remainder of the chapter is as follows. Section 4.2 discusses the empirical model and the data; Section 4.3 presents the empirical results; and Section 4.4 summarizes and concludes the essay.

Chapter II

The Macroeconomic Risks
of Deposit Institutions

SECTION 2.1
THE ARBITRAGE PRICING THEORY (APT)

The Arbitrage Pricing Theory (APT) was originally introduced by Ross [1976, 1977] and later extended by Connor [1982], Huberman [1982], Chen and Ingersoll [1983], Chamberlain and Rothschild [1983], Ingersoll [1984], Wei [1988], and other researchers. The assumptions that are generally employed in the derivation of the APT are:

(a) All investors homogeneously expect that the stochastic properties of capital asset returns are consistent with a linear structure of k factors, i.e., investors believe the following asset return-generating process (the linear factor model),

$$r_i = E_i + b_{i1} f_1 + \ldots + b_{ik} f_k + \epsilon_i , \qquad (2.1.1)$$

where E_i is the expected return on asset i; f_j, $j = 1, \ldots, k$ are the k mean zero factors common to all assets; b_{ij} is the sensitivity of the return on asset i to the change in factor j; and ϵ_i is the idiosyncratic risk of the ith asset with $E(\epsilon_i | f_j) = 0$ for all j;

(b) Either there are no arbitrage opportunities in the capital markets or the capital market is in competitive equilibrium; and

(c) The number of securities in the economy is large enough relative to the number of factors.

Under (a), (b), and (c), the equilibrium expected return on the ith asset is given by,

$$E_i = \lambda_0 + \lambda_1 b_{i1} + \ldots + \lambda_k b_{ik} , \qquad (2.1.2)$$

where λ_0 is the return of a riskless (or a "zero-beta") asset; and $\lambda_1, \lambda_2, \ldots, \lambda_k$ can be interpreted as risk premium parameters associated with risk factors $f_1, f_2, \ldots, f_k$.

There are two major approaches in the empirical investigations of the APT model. The first one started with the seminal paper of Roll and Ross [1980], followed by Brown and Weinstein [1983], Chen [1983], Cho, Elton, and Gruber [1984], Dhrmes, Friend, and Gultekin [1984], and many others. These authors take a two-stage approach, as in Fama and MacBeth [1973]. First, factor analysis is used to estimate the factor sensitivities, i.e., the b_{ij}'s, from the stock returns for firms (and possibly a measure of the risk free rate), and then the estimates of the risk premium parameters, λ_j's, are obtained from cross-sectional regression of the expected return of assets on the estimated b_{ij}'s. Some of the problems with this two-stage approach are:

(1) In factor analysis, the estimated b_{ij}'s are not unique. They can only be determined up to an orthogonal transformation;

(2) The statistical factors and associated λ_j's do not have any *a priori* interpretation; and

(3) In the second stage, the estimated b_{ij}'s contain measurement errors. This will bias the estimates of λ_j's.

The second approach, in attempting to avoid the above problems with the two-stage approach, proposes to use observable economic variables directly in the linear factor model (see McElroy, Burmeister, and Wall [1985] and McElroy and Burmeister [1988]). This strategy follows the tradition of Chan, Chen, and Hsieh [1985] and Chen, Roll, and Ross [1986] and interprets the factors in the linear factor model as unanticipated changes in economic variables which generate unexpected movements in asset prices. As pointed out in McElroy,

Burmeister, and Wall [1985] and McElroy and Burmeister [1988], by replacing the unknown random factors of factor analysis with observed macroeconomic variables, we can recast the APT as a multivariate nonlinear regression model with cross-equational restrictions. The nonlinear seemingly unrelated regression (NLSUR) method can be used to estimate both the factor sensitivities, the b_{ij}'s, and the risk premium parameters, λ_j's, jointly, thus avoiding the above three problems with the two-stage approach of the estimation of the APT.

This study adopts the second approach of empirical investigations of the APT. By putting macroeconomic variables directly into the linear factor model, we can interpret the b_{ij}'s and λ_j's as risk sensitivities and risk premium parameters of the related macroeconomic variables. For example, if an interest rate index appears as one factor in the linear factor model, then the associated b_{ij} will be the interest rate sensitivity and λ_j will be the risk premium parameter for taking interest rate risk. However, the interpretation of the risk premium parameters, λ_j's, needs further explanation.

In Equation 2.1.2, if there is a riskless asset, or a zero-beta asset, with return, E_0, then $b_{0j} = 0$ and

$$E_0 = \lambda_0 .$$

Hence, we obtain,

$$E_i - E_0 = \lambda_1 b_{i1} + ... + \lambda_k b_{ik} . \qquad (2.1.3)$$

By forming portfolios with $b_{ij} = 1$ and $b_{ik} = 0$, $k \neq j$, and letting E^j be the return to the portfolio, then we have,

$$\lambda_j = E^j - E_0 .$$

That is, the risk premium parameter λ_j is the excess return of the portfolio with one unit risk of jth factor and zero risks of other factors. An explanation for λ_j is given in Roll and Ross

[1980]. By adopting an intertemporal diffusion model, they show that, for a given preference,

$$\lambda_j = E^j - E_0 = [\Sigma_1 w_1 R_1 \, (1/c_1) \, (\partial c_1/\partial s_j)] \, \sigma_j^2 . \qquad (2.1.4)$$

where 1 indexes individual agents, w_1 is the proportion of total wealth held by agent 1, R_1 is her coefficient of relative risk aversion, $(1/c_1) \, (\partial c_1/\partial s_j)$ is the partial elasticity of her consumption with respect to changes in the jth factor, and σ_j^2 is the variance of the jth factor (see details in Appendix E). We can draw two conclusions from the above expression for λ_j: the larger the variance of the factor j, the larger the associated risk premium parameter; and, if the partial elasticity of consumption of all agents with respect to the jth factor is zero, the risk premium parameter, λ_j, is zero. Note that λ_j can be negative if all the partial elasticities are negative.

One advantage of the APT is that the pricing relationship (see Equation 2.1.2) can be derived by considering any set of n assets which follows the factor-generating process (see Equation 2.1.1). The essential condition of the APT pricing relationship is that no arbitrage opportunity exists. This holds even in a subset of the universe of assets, as long as the number of assets is large enough relative to the number of factors, allowing the law of large numbers to hold true.

Bower, Bower, and Logue [1984] and Pettway and Jordan [1987] apply the APT to public utility industry stocks and show that it provides both a better indication of asset risk and a better estimate of expected return than the one-period Capital Asset Pricing Model (CAPM). Sweeney and Warga [1986] suggest that interest rate risk is priced in the sense of the APT by looking at stock returns of the utility industry only. This study is the first attempt to apply the idea of the APT to deposit-institution stock returns in order to study the macroeconomic risk exposures of deposit institutions.

SECTION 2.2
MODEL SPECIFICATION AND
ESTIMATION METHOD

To write the APT as a multivariate regression model for a sample of N assets, Equation 2.1.2 is substituted into Equation 2.1.1 to obtain a system of N nonlinear regressions over T time periods.

$$r_i(t) = \lambda_0 + \sum_{j=1}^{K} b_{ij} \lambda_j + \sum_{j=1}^{K} b_{ij} f_j(t) + \epsilon_i(t), \quad (2.2.1)$$
$$i=1, ..., N \text{ and } t=1, ..., T.$$

There are $N*(K+1)$ parameters in this system (λ_j's and b_{ij}'s) to be estimated. The term $\sum_{j=1}^{K} b_{ij} \lambda_j$ is a parametric representation of N-K nonlinear cross-equational restrictions expressing the N intercepts of Equation 2.1.1 in terms of the K parameters, λ_1, ..., λ_K. The terms $f_j(t)$ and $j=1,...,K$ are K directly observable macroeconomic variables. To use directly observed macroeconomic variables in Equation 2.2.1 is not inconsistent with the APT since the factors in Equation 2.1.1 need not be the factors from factor analysis. Actually, factors need not be orthogonal or normalized. In addition, as shown by the work of Chamberlain and Rothschild [1983], Ingersoll [1984], and Grinblatt and Titman [1985], the idiosyncratic disturbances do not have to be uncorrelated for the APT to hold (for example, as shown by Chamberlain and Rothschild [1984], the APT still holds true if the eigenvalues of the residual matrix are uniformly bounded).

Under this interpretation of the $f_j(t)$'s, Equation 2.2.1 is a multivariate nonlinear regression model with cross-equational restrictions for which McElroy, Burmeister, and Wall [1985] show that, conditional on the factor realizations, Gallant's [1975] nonlinear seemingly unrelated regression (NLSUR) technique can be used to obtain joint estimators for the b_{ij}'s and λ_j's. The detailed steps for estimating Equation 2.2.1 are explained in

Appendix A. In general, the NLSUR minimizes a generalized sum of squares of the following form of objective values,

$$r'(S^{-1} \otimes I)r/n$$

where

$$r = \begin{bmatrix} r_1 \\ r_2 \\ . \\ . \\ . \\ r_N \end{bmatrix}$$

is the nNX1 vector of residuals for the N equations stacked together.

S is an NXN matrix that estimates Σ, the covariance of the errors across equations.

These NLSUR estimators from Appendix A, even without the normality of the error distribution (which is important since the normality assumption of asset returns is questionable), are strongly consistent and asymptotically normal, and they form the basis for classical asymptotic hypothesis testing. If, in addition, the errors are multivariate normal, the iterated NLSUR (ITNLSUR) gives full information maximum likelihood estimators (FIML). The cross-sectional restrictions implied by the APT can be tested by invoking the chi-square test where the χ^2 value equals the difference between the objective value of the restricted model and the nonrestricted linear model times N, and the degree of freedom equals the difference in the number of free parameters in the two models (see Gallant and Jorgenson [1979]).

The model specification in Equation 2.2.1 assumes that all K factors are observable. However, in practice, there may be some unobserved factors in the linear factor model. To deal with this possibility, I follow McElroy and Burmeister [1988] and assume that in Equation 2.2.1, the first J = K-1 factors are observed, but the Kth factor is unobserved and, therefore, is part of the error term,

$$u_i(t) = b_{ik} f_k(t) + \epsilon_i(t), \quad i=1, ..., n, \quad (2.2.2)$$

where $f_k(t)$ is an unobserved shock common to all returns at time t (e.g., "market psychology," "rumors of war," etc.), b_{ik} is the sensitivity of returns of the ith asset to that common shock, and $\epsilon_i(t)$ is, as before, an asset-specific shock or idiosyncratic noise. I continue to assume that this K^{th} factor is mean zero, constant variance, serially uncorrelated, and uncorrelated with the idiosyncratic noise. In addition, I assume that this K^{th} factor is uncorrelated with the observed factors for all t and $t' = 1,..,T$,

$$E[f_K(t) f_j(t')] = 0, \quad j=1, ..., J.$$

As before, the reward for taking a unit of factor-K risk is λ_K.

Assuming that there exists a well-diversified portfolio (with zero idiosyncratic noise) with return $r_m = \sum_{i=1}^{m} w_i r_i$, given by the aggregation of Equation 2.1.1 to,

$$r_m(t) = \lambda_0(t) + \lambda_m + \sum_{j=1}^{J} b_{mj} f_j(t) + b_{mk} f_k(t) + \epsilon(t),$$

where $w_1, ..., w_m$ are portfolio weights summing to one, $b_{mj} = \sum_{i=1}^{m} w_1 b_{ij}$, for $j = 1, ..., K$, $\epsilon_m(t) = \sum_{i=1}^{m} w_i \epsilon_i(t)$, and var $\epsilon_m(t)$ = o (zero idiosyncratic noise), $\epsilon_m(t)$ is a degenerate random variable at zero. Since $f_K(t)$ is unobserved and b_{mk} is not identified, without loss of generality I normalize $f_K(t)$ such that $b_{mk} = 1$. Thus,

$$r_m(t) = \lambda_0(t) + \lambda_m + \sum_{j=1}^{J} b_{mj} f_j(t) + f_K(t), \quad t=1, ..., T.$$
$$(2.2.3)$$

Since the unobserved factor, $f_K(t)$, is simply the error term in Equation 2.2.3, in using OLS to Equation 2.2.3, the least square residual yields a consistent estimator $\hat{f}_K$ (t) of the factor f_K (t). In Equation 2.2.1, adding and subtracting f_K(t) gives,

$$r_i (t) = \lambda_0 + \sum_{j=1}^{J} b_{ij} \lambda_j + b_{iK}\lambda_K + \sum_{j=1}^{J} b_{ij} f_j (t) + b_{ik} \hat{f}_K (t) + e_i (t),$$
$$i=1, ..., N \text{ and } t=1, ..., T , \qquad\qquad (2.2.4)$$

where,

$$e_i (t) = \epsilon (t) + b_{iK} (f_K (t) - \hat{f}_K (t))$$
$$= \epsilon_i (t) + b_{iK} [\lambda_m - \hat{\lambda}_m + \sum_{j=1}^{J} (b_{mj} - \hat{b}_{mj})] ,$$

where the "hats" indicate the OLS estimators from Equation 2.2.3. In Section 2.5, Equation 2.2.4 is estimated by NLSUR.

SECTION 2.3
THE SAMPLE DATA

The sample data for the dependent variables in Equation 2.2.1 is taken from the Center for Research in Security Prices (CRSP) at the University of Chicago. All 33 commercial banks and savings and loan associations are selected for which the CRSP tape shows monthly returns from June, 1976 to December, 1987. The sample deposit institutions and their asset sizes of 1982 are shown in Table 1. In order to test for possible intra-industry differences in risk sensitivities and risk premiums, the deposit institutions are further divided into three different groups: money-center banks (determined by Citibank's competitors list; see Sinkey [1986]), regional banks, and S&L's. Monthly stock return data is chosen because, for the purpose of estimating the APT, the relevant macroeconomic variables are collected and compiled for monthly intervals.

The macroeconomic variables chosen for this study are similar to those of Chen, Roll and Ross [1986]. They use the discounted cash-flow formula to suggest that the four

Table 1

The sample banks and savings and loan associations

Institution	Asset Size (Million $ at End of 1984)
Money-Center Banks	
1. BankAmerica Corp.	117,680
2. Bankers Trust of New York Corp.	45,208
3. Chase Manhattan Corp.	86,883
4. Chemical Bank of New York City	52,236
5. Citicorp	150,586
6. Continental Bank of Illinois Corp.	30,413
7. First Chicago Corp.	39,846
8. Manufacturers Hanover Corp.	75,713
9. J.P. Morgan and Co., Inc.	64,126
Regional Banks	
1. Bank of Boston	22,079
2. Bank of New York, Inc.	15,156
3. First Interstate Bancorp, Inc.	17,318
4. Irving Bank Corp.	18,982
5. Marine Midland Banks, Inc.	22,056
6. NBD Bancorp, Inc.	14,232
7. Norwest Corp.	21,346
8. Southeast Banking Corp.	9,869
9. Wells Fargo and Co.	28,184
10. Bank of Virginia	4,134
11. Equimark Corp.	2,593
12. First Pennsylvania Corp.	5,355
13. First Virginia Banks, Inc.	2,686
14. First Wisconsin Corp.	5,516
Savings and Loan Associations	
1. Ahmanson H.F. & Co.	24,307
2. Far West Financial Corp.	2,050
3. Financial Corporation of America	28,518
4. Gibraltar Financial Corp.	9,273
5. Golden West Financial Corp., DFL	10,620
6. Great Western Financial Corp.	23,555
7. Imperial Corporation of America	8,465
8. TransOhio Financial Corp.	2,797
9. Financial Corporation, Santa Barbara	2,094
10. Signet Banking Corporation	1,910

macroeconomic variables--the interest rate index as proxied by
the difference in the return on the long-term government bond
and the one-month treasury bill, the expected and unexpected
inflation, industrial production, and the spread between high- and
low-grade bonds--systematically affect stock market returns. In
addition, they find that these four macroeconomic factors are
priced in the sense of the APT for stock returns. This study
examines whether the deposit-institution stock returns are
sensitive to these economic variables and whether the
macroeconomic variables are priced.

The first macroeconomic factor is an interest rate factor,
which is the difference between the returns of a portfolio of
long-term government bonds and the one-month treasury bill.

$$f_1 (t) \;=\; UTS (t) \;=\; LGB (t) - TB (t-1) \;,$$

where LGB (t) is the return on the long-term government bonds
obtained from Ibbotson Associates [1988], and TB (t) refers to
the return on the one-month treasury bill. Under the assumption
of the appropriate form of risk neutrality, E $(f_1 (t)) = 0$. This
variable can be thought of as a measure of the unanticipated
return on the interest rate factor. Deposit institutions are believed
to be subject to interest rate risk due to the "short" position of
the asset and liability structure, i.e., the maturity of the asset is
longer than that of the liability.

The second macroeconomic variable is the default risk
premia factor, defined as,

$$f_2 (t) \;=\; UPR (t) \;=\; LCB (t) - LGB (t) \;,$$

where LCB (t) is the return on the long-term corporate bond
from Ibbotson Associates [1988]. The government bond is
default-free, while the corporate bond is not. Therefore, the
investors need compensation for holding a corporate bond instead
of a government bond. Although UPR is not formally an
innovation, as the difference in two return series it is sufficiently

uncorrelated that we can treat it as an innovation. A check of the sample autocorrelations assures this assertion. The UPR variable would have mean zero in a risk-neutral world, and it can be thought of as a measure of the degree of risk aversion implicit in pricing. As suggested by Chan, Chen and Hsieh [1985], the business risk and, hence, the risk premia factor may vary with changing business conditions. The default risk premia factor might affect the deposit institutions since the banking business is closely related to the business cycle of the economy.

The third macroeconomic factor is an unexpected inflation series, defined as,

$$f_3 (t) = UI (t) = I(t) - E [I (t)|t-1] ,$$

where I (t) is the realized monthly first difference in the logarithm of the Consumer Price Index (CPI) and E [I (t)|t-1] is the expected inflation calculated from the real interest-rate model of Fama and Gibbons [1984] (see details in Appendix D). The reasons for adopting this unexpected inflation index are twofold. First, as shown by Fama and Gibbons [1984], the real interest-rate model gives us a better forecast for inflation than simple ARMA models. For the sample data used, Q-tests reject simple ARIMA models with reasonable AR and MA terms). Second, the unexpected inflation variable also represents the unexpected real return of investment which has every reason to affect the stock returns.

The fourth macroeconomic factor is the log-difference of the monthly industrial index. That is,

$$f_4 (t) = IPI (t) = \log (IP_{t+1}/IP_t) .$$

IPI (t) represents the current level of real economic activity. Some previous studies suggest that bank stocks are related to a change in industrial production (see p. 59, Ch. 2, Benston, Eisenbeis, Horvitz, Kane, and Kaufman). A sharp downturn in the stock market is often associated with a sharp decline in industrial production. As argued by Chen, Roll, and Ross [1988], the change in the industrial production index is noisy enough to be treated as an innovation. An examination of the sample autocorrelation of f_4 (t) confirms this assertion.

Finally, the market index, r_m (t), is taken as the total return on the CRSP equally-weighted stock return. The residual market factor, which serves as a proxy for the unexpected return, ER (t), is the residual of the following regression equation,

$$\hat{r}_m - \lambda_0 = 0.0076 + 0.3909 \text{ UTS} - 0.0324 \text{ UPR} +$$
$$\phantom{\hat{r}_m - \lambda_0 = } (1.70) \quad\quad (0.97) \quad\quad\quad (2.07)$$

$$0.1729 \text{ UI} - 0.0717 \text{ IPI.}$$
$$(0.09) \quad\quad\quad (0.35)$$

The numbers in parentheses are t-statistics, $R^2 = 0.05$. The intercept 0.0076 is lower than the sample excess return of the market return 0.0085. The market index is negatively related to the default risk premia factor and the change in industrial production but positively related to the interest rate factor and the unexpected inflation factor. The coefficient on the default risk premia is significant at the standard level. Together, the four macroeconomic variables explain only about 5 percent of the variation of the excess return on the CRSP equally-weighted stock index.

The sample mean and correlations of the four macroeconomic variables and the residual market factor are reported in Table 2. As seen in the table, the sample correlations between the interest rate factor and the other three macroeconomic variables are negative. By construction, all four macroeconomic variables are unrelated to the residual market factor, ER.

Table 2

Sample mean, autocorrelations, and correlations of the four economic factors,
UTS (t), UPR (t), UI (t), IPI (t), and ER (t)

	UTS (t)	UPR (t)	UI (t)	IPI (t)	ER (t)
Mean	0.0017	0.0004	-0.0001	0.0000	0.0000
Std. dev.	0.0377	0.0119	0.0026	0.0222	0.0512
Correlation					
UTS (t)	1.0000	-0.3757	-0.2971	-0.1718	0.0000
UPR (t)		1.0000	0.3142	0.1433	0.0000
UI (t)			1.0000	0.1429	0.0000
IPI (t)				1.0000	0.0000
ER (t)					1.0000

UTS is the difference in the return of the long-term government bond from Ibbotson Associates [1988]; UPR is the difference between the return of the long-term corporate bond and the long-term government bond; UI is the unexpected inflation from the real interest rate model of Fama and Gibbons [1984]; IPI is the log difference in the industrial production index; and ER is the residual market factor.

SECTION 2.4
EMPIRICAL RESULTS

The Iterated Nonlinear Seemingly Unrelated Estimates (ITNLSUR) is computed for the system in Equation 2.2.4. The four macroeconomic factor measures and the residual market return proved to be important in explaining 30 to 40 percent of the variations in most of the returns of the sample deposit-institution stocks. Figures 1-3 compare the fitted values of the expected returns from the model and the actual excess returns for BankAmerica (one of the money-center banks), the Bank of Boston (one of the regional banks), and TransOhio Financial Corporation (one of the S&L's). It seems that the fitted values trace the variations of the actual returns rather well.

Table 3 reports the ITNLSUR estimates of the risk premium parameter λ's. The risk premium parameters for the interest rate factor and the industrial production factor are significant at the 0.05 level. The risk premium parameters for the default risk premia factor and the residual market factor are marginally significant at p-values of 0.13 and 0.09, respectively. Finally, the risk premium parameter for the unexpected inflation factor is statistically insignificant. While the risk premium parameters for the interest rate factor and the residual market factor are positive, the rest of the factors have negative risk premium parameters. The p-value for the test of the cross-sectional constraint implied by the APT is 0.45, which does not reject the test.

To determine whether an economic factor contributes to the total risk premium--the difference between a deposit-institution stock return and a risk-free rate--one also needs to know whether the deposit-institution stock returns are sensitive to that economic factor. The results of the factor sensitivities, b_{ij}'s, are reported in Table 4.

Table 4 reports the ITNLSUR estimates of the b_{ij}'s of the APT and their asymptotic t-ratios. All of the factor sensitivities

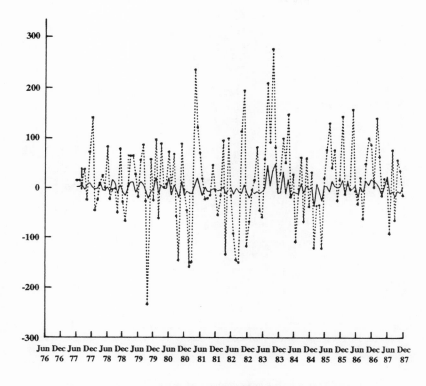

Figure 1. The Fitted and Actual Values of the Stock Returns
for BankAmerica Corp.

——— The fitted return
***** The actual return

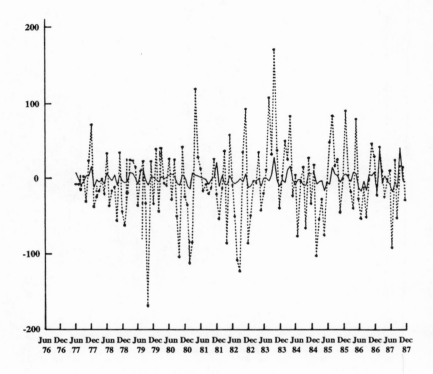

Figure 2. The Fitted and Actual Values of the Stock Returns
for Bank of Boston.

——— The fitted return
***** The actual return

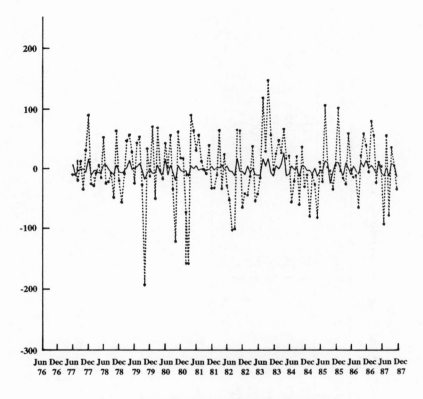

Figure 3. The Fitted and Actual Values of the Stock Returns
for TransOhio Corp.

——— The fitted return
***** The actual return

Table 3

Estimates of the risk premium parameters, λ's

Parameter	Estimate	t-statistic	Prob. Value
UTS	0.0058	2.32	0.0217
UPR	-0.0067	-1.54	0.1255
UI	-0.0005	-0.66	0.5078
IPI	-0.0022	-2.77	0.0065
R_m	0.0028	1.81	0.0727

Chi-square test of the cross-sectional restrictions

X^2 (29) = 28.00

p-value = 0.45

UTS, UPR, UI, IPI, and R_m represent the interest rate factor, the default risk premia factor, unexpected inflation, the change in industrial production factor, and the residual market factor, respectively. The X^2 test is a test of cross-sectional restrictions on the linear factor model implied by the APT.

Table 4
Estimates of the factor sensitivities, b_{ij}'s
(t-statistics are in parentheses)

Firm No. i	b_{i1} (UTS)	b_{i2} (UPR)	b_{i3} (UI)	b_{i4} (IPI)	b_{i5} (R_m)	R^2
Money-Center Banks						
1.	1.12* (5.56)	0.96 (1.49)	3.04 (1.06)	0.55* (2.37)	0.67* (4.97)	0.41
2.	1.02* (7.06)	0.91 (1.98)	1.73 (0.84)	0.00 (0.02)	0.86* (9.02)	0.47
3.	0.81* (5.28)	-0.22 (0.45)	4.99* (2.27)	0.07 (0.42)	0.90* (8.76)	0.47
4.	0.71* (4.75)	0.16 (0.33)	2.19 (1.02)	0.07 (0.41)	0.78* (7.82)	0.29
5.	0.90* (6.70)	-0.15 (0.36)	2.16 (1.13)	0.27 (1.65)	0.92* (10.31)	0.49
6.	0.67* (2.07)	0.21 (0.20)	-0.86 (0.19)	0.29 (0.85)	1.00* (4.65)	0.45

Table 4 (cont.)

7.	0.55* (2.73)	0.47 (0.72)	-2.71 (0.94)	0.04 (0.17)	0.97* (7.24)	0.38
8.	0.94* (3.84)	2.31* (2.94)	-6.71 (1.92)	-0.32 (1.15)	1.13* (6.93)	0.54
9.	2.03* (5.11)	1.71 (1.34)	-11.45 (2.02)	0.33 (0.73)	1.37* (5.19)	0.17
Average	0.97	0.71	-0.85	0.14	0.96	
Regional Banks						
10.	0.76* (4.48)	0.15 (0.28)	3.65 (1.52)	0.06 (0.32)	0.98* (8.77)	0.31
11.	1.06* (7.83)	1.57* (3.61)	1.66 (0.86)	0.03 (0.21)	0.77* (8.51)	0.35
12.	1.00* (4.11)	2.30* (2.95)	8.79* (2.54)	-0.13 (0.45)	0.96* (5.94)	0.32
13.	0.70* (4.56)	1.10* (2.24)	-0.14 (0.06)	-0.28 (1.61)	0.85* (8.31)	0.42
14.	0.41* (2.66)	0.25 (0.52)	-1.85 (0.85)	-0.26 (1.56)	0.77* (7.54)	0.49

Table 4 *(cont.)*

15.	0.75* (5.78)	0.75 (1.81)	1.39 (0.76)	-0.18 (1.21)	0.71* (8.21)	0.32
16.	2.17* (8.14)	1.81* (2.11)	0.89 (0.23)	0.52 (1.65)	1.51* (8.53)	0.41
17.	2.01* (8.19)	2.25* (2.86)	0.61 (0.17)	0.25 (0.86)	1.07* (6.57)	0.33
18.	1.85* (9.59)	1.14 (1.86)	4.15 (1.52)	0.43 (1.77)	0.87* (6.78)	0.43
19.	1.59* (6.24)	-0.06 (0.07)	0.41 (0.11)	0.44 (1.52)	1.26* (7.44)	0.51
20.	0.28* (1.56)	-0.26 (0.45)	-1.18 (0.46)	-0.35 (1.74)	0.71* (5.89)	0.45
21.	0.95* (5.83)	0.29 (0.56)	2.77 (1.19)	0.39* (2.16)	0.62* (5.67)	0.51
22.	0.64* (3.33)	-0.49 (0.80)	0.02 (0.01)	-0.18 (0.82)	0.95* (7.43)	0.43
23.	0.73* (5.19)	-0.04 (0.10)	3.50 (1.74)	0.11 (0.72)	0.62* (6.59)	0.24
Average	1.06	0.76	1.76	0.06	0.90	

Table 4 (cont.)

S&L's

24.	0.67* (5.15)	0.25 (0.59)	2.36 (1.29)	-0.13 (0.91)	0.68* (7.92)	0.33
25.	0.74* (5.20)	0.54 (1.18)	2.96 (1.45)	0.00 (0.03)	0.81* (8.47)	0.34
26.	0.76* (5.65)	0.84 (1.95)	-1.07 (0.56)	-0.02 (0.12)	0.68* (7.68)	0.35
27.	0.56* (4.08)	0.28 (0.62)	-0.49 (0.25)	-0.15 (0.95)	0.88* (9.45)	0.41
28.	1.04* (4.68)	1.50* (2.09)	0.02 (0.01)	-0.03 (0.12)	1.19* (8.04)	0.42
29.	0.69* (4.76)	1.18* (2.51)	-2.19 (1.05)	-0.22 (1.32)	0.60* (6.15)	0.40
30.	1.09* (7.43)	0.06 (0.13)	5.69* (2.74)	0.17 (0.97)	0.76* (0.84)	0.45
31.	1.84* (7.30)	1.74* (2.14)	0.99 (0.28)	0.27 (0.95)	1.06* (6.33)	0.39
32.	0.75* (5.29)	-0.08 (0.17)	3.39 (1.69)	-0.12 (0.71)	0.88* (9.34)	0.34

Table 4 *(cont.)*

33.	0.80* (6.21)	0.14 (0.34)	-0.34 (0.18)	0.09 (0.65)	0.75* (8.74)	0.47
Average	0.89	0.65	1.13	-0.01	0.83	

The symbols, b_{i1}, b_{i2}, b_{i3}, b_{i4}, and b_{i5} are the risk sensitivities of the ith deposit institution to the interest rate factor, the default risk premia factor, the unexpected inflation, the change in industrial production factor, and the residual market factor, respectively. The * represents that the coefficient is significant at the 0.05 level.

associated with the interest rate factor and the residual market factor are positive, and all of them are significant at the 0.05 level. Less than one-third of deposit-institution stocks are sensitive to the default risk premia factor. Most of the factor sensitivities for the unexpected changes in the inflation factor and the industrial production factor are statistically insignificant.

Specifically, only five out of 33 factor sensitivities are significant for the unexpected inflation factor, and merely two out of 33 factor sensitivities are significant for the industrial production factor. The interesting result is that, although from Table 2 we know that the risk premium parameter is significant for the industrial production factor, the sample deposit-institution stocks are not sensitive to the factor. The net contributions of the industrial production factor to the total risk premiums of deposit-institution stocks, the $b_{ij}\lambda_j$'s, are insignificant. Different deposit institutions are subject to different levels of both interest rate risk and market risk, ranging from 0.28 to 2.03 and 0.62 to 1.37, respectively. Table 4 also calculates the average betas for the three groups of deposit institutions: money-center banks, regional banks, and S&L's. The money-center banks have an average interest rate beta of 0.97; the regional banks have an average interest rate beta of 1.06; and the S&L's have an average interest rate beta of 0.89. The beta for the residual market factor is highest for the money-center banks (0.96) and lowest for the S&L's (0.83), with the regional banks in between (0.90). The betas for the default risk premia factor are not much different for the three groups of deposit institutions. However, money-center banks tend to have a negative beta for the unexpected inflation factor, while the regional banks and the S&L's have positive betas. Finally, the betas for the unexpected inflation factor are quite small for all three groups of deposit institutions. The average beta for the money-center banks is 0.14, and the regional banks and S&L's have even smaller average betas of 0.06 and -0.01, respectively.

Although this study does not exhaust all relevant macroeconomic variables, a set of macroeconomic variables believed to be important in affecting deposit-institution stock returns is explored. The fact that deposit-institution stock returns tend to be more sensitive to the interest rate and residual market factors partially explains the popularity of the two-index market model--with a market index and an interest rate index--in studying the issue of the riskiness of banking. In the following discussion, the implied total risk premia, the component contributions of the four macroeconomic factors, and the residual market factor are calculated from the estimated APT model for deposit-institution stock returns.

Table 5 reports the total risk premia and the component contributions of the interest rate factor, the default risk premia factor, the unexpected inflation factor, and the change in industrial production factor. The average total risk premia (monthly) for the money-center banks, the regional banks, and the S&L's are 0.79%, 0.72%, and 0.65%, respectively. The risk premiums for the interest rate factor account for approximately 70% of the total risk premia; they are 0.56%, 0.56%, and 0.52% for the three groups of deposit institutions. The risk premiums for the residual market factor are 0.27%, 0.26%, and 0.23% for the three groups of deposit institutions; they account for approximately 30% of the total risk premia. The risk premiums for the remainder of the macroeconomic factors are small relative to the contributions of the interest rate factor and the residual market factor. The risk premiums for the default risk premia factor are negative for all three groups of deposit institutions; they are -0.05%, -0.05%, and -0.04%, respectively. Regarding the unexpected inflation factor, the risk premium for the money-center banks is 0.05, while the risk premiums for both the regional banks and the S&L's are negative at -0.08% and -0.06%, respectively. Finally, while the regional banks and S&L's have zero risk premiums, the money-center banks have a negative risk premium (-0.03% for the change in industrial production factor). The negative risk premiums for the default risk premia and unexpected inflation factors suggest that deposit-institution stocks may be hedges against these risks. Zero

Table 5

The total risk premia and component contributions ($b_{ij}\lambda_j$) of the four macroeconomic factors and the residual market factor (monthly, %).

Firm No.	Total Risk Premia ($\Sigma b_{ij}\lambda_j$)	UTS ($b_{i1}\lambda_1$)	UPR ($b_{i2}\lambda_2$)	UI ($b_{i3}\lambda_3$)	IPI ($b_{i4}\lambda_4$)	ER ($b_{i5}\lambda_5$)
Money-Center Banks						
1.	0.49	0.65	-0.06	-0.15	-0.12	0.18
2.	0.68	0.59	-0.06	-0.08	0.00	0.24
3.	0.48	0.47	0.01	-0.25	-0.01	0.25
4.	0.49	0.41	-0.01	-0.10	-0.01	0.21
5.	0.62	0.52	0.01	-0.10	-0.06	0.26
6.	0.63	0.38	-0.01	0.04	-0.06	0.28
7.	0.69	0.32	-0.03	0.14	0.00	0.27
8.	1.11	0.55	-0.16	0.34	0.07	0.32
9.	1.94	1.17	-0.12	0.57	-0.07	0.38
Average	0.79	0.56	-0.05	0.05	-0.03	0.27
Regional Banks						
10.	0.51	0.44	-0.01	-0.18	-0.01	0.27

Table 5 *(cont.)*

11.	0.63	0.61	-0.11	-0.08	0.00	0.26
12.	0.28	0.58	-0.16	-0.44	0.03	0.27
13.	0.63	0.41	-0.07	0.07	0.06	0.24
14.	0.59	0.24	-0.02	0.09	0.06	0.22
15.	0.55	0.44	-0.05	-0.07	0.04	0.19
16.	1.39	1.26	-0.13	-0.04	-0.11	0.43
17.	1.22	1.17	-0.16	-0.03	-0.05	0.29
18.	0.93	1.07	-0.08	-0.21	-0.09	0.24
19.	1.16	0.09	0.00	-0.02	-0.09	0.36
20.	0.52	0.16	0.01	0.06	0.07	0.19
21.	0.48	0.55	-0.02	-0.14	-0.08	0.17
22.	0.71	0.37	0.03	0.00	0.04	0.27
23.	0.41	0.42	0.00	-0.17	-0.02	0.17
Average	0.72	0.56	-0.05	-0.08	0.00	0.26
S&L's						
24.	0.47	0.39	-0.01	-0.12	0.03	0.19
25.	0.47	0.43	-0.04	-0.14	0.00	0.23
26.	0.63	0.44	-0.06	0.05	0.00	0.19
27.	0.61	0.33	-0.02	0.02	0.03	0.25
28.	0.84	0.60	-0.10	0.00	0.00	0.33
29.	0.64	0.40	-0.08	0.11	0.04	0.17
30.	0.51	0.63	0.00	-0.28	-0.03	0.21
31.	1.13	1.06	-0.12	-0.05	-0.06	0.29

Table 5 (cont.)

32.	0.54	0.44	0.00	-0.17	0.02	0.25
33.	0.66	0.46	0.00	0.02	-0.02	0.21
Average	0.65	0.52	-0.04	-0.06	0.00	0.23

risk premiums for the industrial production factor suggest that investors in deposit-institution stocks are not very concerned about the risk. Since market participants tend to have a better understanding of the risk conditions of a deposit institution, the risk premium for which they ask to be compensated provides useful information, enabling government regulators to price deposit insurance and set capital standard.

SECTION 2.5
SUMMARY AND FURTHER RESEARCH PLANS

Deposit institutions have long been believed to be subject to macroeconomic risks. This study examines the macroeconomic risk exposures of a sample of deposit institutions by applying the Arbitrage Pricing Theory. Four macroeconomic variables--the interest rate factor as proxied by the difference in the return of the long-term government bond portfolio and the one-month treasury bill, the default risk premia factor as represented by the difference in the return of a long-term corporate bond portfolio and a portfolio of the long-term government bond, the unexpected inflation factor, and the change in industrial production factor--similar to those chosen by Chen, Roll, and Ross [1986], were investigated to see whether they affected deposit-institution stock returns. I found that all the sample deposit-institution stock returns examined in this study are sensitive to both the interest rate factor and the residual market factor. Less than one-third of the sample deposit-institution stock returns is sensitive to the default risk premia factor and almost all the deposit-institution stock returns are insensitive either to the unexpected inflation factor or the change in industrial production factor. It was further found that, among the four macroeconomic variables, only the interest rate factor is strongly priced in the sense of the APT. The risk premiums for the interest rate factor consist of the largest shares of the total risk premia, which confirms the importance of the interest rate risk in banking research. The implied total risk premia and the risk premiums for the five factors from the APT model also provide useful information in pricing deposit insurance since investors in deposit-institution stocks tend to have better information than regulators about the risks of deposit institutions.

One assumption made in this study is that both the expected returns and betas are constant over the sample period. This assumption can be relaxed by adopting the ARCH modeling strategy to the multi-factor model, an idea which is further pursued in Chapter III. Other potential extensions include exploring different macroeconomic variables and relating macroeconomic risks of deposit institutions to risks measured from a deposit-institution balance sheet, an idea further pursued in Chapter IV. Risks identified in this study can also be related to risk measures (e.g., the CAMEL rating, where *CAMEL* refers to "Capital, Assets, Management, Earnings, and Liquidity") currently adopted by U.S. bank regulators. These works can be attempted in a further study.

Chapter III

The Two-Factor ARCH Model for Deposit-Institution Stocks

SECTION 3.1
THE MULTI-FACTOR ASSET PRICING MODEL

Merton [1973] develops an Intertemporal Capital Asset Pricing Model (ICAPM) to derive a multi-factor model. He assumes that investors can trade continuously in time and maximize the expected utility of their lifetime consumption. Allowing for a stochastic investment opportunity set, he obtains a multi-beta Capital Asset Pricing Model,

$$(R_k - r) = \sum_I \beta_{ik} (R_i - r) , \qquad (3.1.1)$$

where R_i is the return on the ith mutual fund, β_{ik} is the instantaneous multiple regression coefficient between the return on the kth security and the return on the ith mutual fund, m is the number of mutual funds necessary to span the space of optimal portfolios held by the investors, and r is the riskless return. The mutual funds identified in the model might be the "market" portfolio and other hedging portfolios for unanticipated changes in the investor's investment opportunity set. Merton focuses on the interest rate and argues that one can take the interest rate as a single instrumental variable to represent the shifts in the investment opportunity set. In this case, the simplified pricing model becomes a two-factor model with market factor and interest rate factor (also see Shanken [1989]).

39

Long [1974] extends Merton's multi-beta model to the multi-good case in a discrete-time economy and shows that stock prices are closely related to inflation and the term structure of interest rates. Breeden [1979] shows that Merton's multi-beta pricing equation can be collapsed into a single-beta equation, where the instantaneous expected return on any security is proportional to its beta (or covariance) with respect to aggregate consumption alone. Cox, Ingersoll, and Ross [1985] develop a continuous-time general equilibrium model of a simple but complete economy and use it to examine the behavior of asset prices. One principal result is a partial differential equation which asset prices must satisfy. The solution of this equation gives the equilibrium price of any asset in terms of the underlying real variables in the economy. A multi-factor model might also be consistent with Sharp's [1977] multi-beta Capital Asset Pricing Model (CAPM) where the market beta of the Sharpe-Linter-Mossin CAPM is expressed as a weighted average of beta values relative to any desired number of portfolios, the collection of which equals the market portfolio.

As the test of the CAPM can be viewed as a test of the conditional mean-variance efficiency of the market portfolio (see, for example, Fama [1976], Roll [1977], and Ross [1977]), the test of a multi-factor asset pricing model can be viewed as a test of the conditional mean-variance efficiency of a combination of specified factors (see Chamberlain [1983], Grinblatt and Titman [1987], Huberman, Kandel, and Stambaugh [1987], Kandel and Stambaugh [1987], and Harvey [1988]). However, this study does not seek to test a multi-factor model. Instead, Merton's version of a multi-factor model is utilized and measures of the risks implied by the model are estimated.

A two-factor model--with market factor and interest rate factor--is applied. The reasons for studying the two-factor model are:

(1) Previous studies suggest that deposit-institution stock returns are closely related to both market factor and interest rate factor (see, for example, Lynge and Zumwalt [1980], Chance

and Lane [1980], Flannery and James [1984], Giliberto [1985], and Kane and Unal [1988]);

(2) The inclusion of the market portfolio and interest rate factor can be justified by Merton's Intertemporal CAPM. (The interest rate factor is believed to be the important factor affecting the investment opportunity set; and

(3) The work in Chapter II suggests that the interest rate factor is priced in the sense of the APT for deposit-institution stock returns.

SECTION 3.2
MODEL SPECIFICATION AND ESTIMATION

Following Bodurtha and Mark [1987] and Mark [1988], the two-factor model of deposit institutions in a conditional environment is specified, where the betas--which are the ratios of a conditional covariance and a conditional variance--are parameterized, following the ARCH modeling strategy. It is assumed that,

$$r_i(t) = E_{t-1}[r_i(t)] + u_t^i, \qquad (3.2.1)$$
$$f_1(t) = E_{t-1}[f_1(t)] + \epsilon_t, \qquad (3.3.2)$$
$$f_2(t) = E_{t-1}[f_2(t)] + \omega_t, \qquad (3.3.3)$$

where $r_i(t)$, $(i = 1, 2, 3)$ are the excess returns and the portfolio return minus the risk-free rate for the three deposit-institution stock portfolios to be discussed in Section 3.3. The values $f_1(t)$ and $f_2(t)$ are the excess returns for the market and interest rate factors of deposit-institution stock returns. The values u_t^i, ϵ_t, and ω_t are the one-step-ahead forecast errors of $r_i(t)$, $f_1(t)$, and $f_2(t)$, respectively.

Without loss of generality, the second factor is assumed to be uncorrelated with the market factor.[1] In a conditional environment, the two-factor model can be specified as,

$$E_{t-1} (r_i (t)) = \frac{Cov_{t-1} (r_i (t), f_1 (t))}{Var_{t-1} (f_1 (t))} E_{t-1} (f_1 (t)) +$$

$$\frac{Cov_{t-1} (r_i (t), f_2 (t))}{Var_{t-1} (f_2 (t))} E_{t-1} (f_2 (t)) \cdot \qquad (3.2.4)$$

The two ratios of conditional covariance and conditional variance represent the market beta and the interest rate beta, respectively. By definition, they depend on the conditional information and, hence, are time-varying. Using Equations 3.2.1, 3.2.2, and 3.2.3, one has,

$$
\begin{aligned}
Cov_{t-1} (r_i(t), f_1(t)) &= E_{t-1} [r_i(t) - E_{t-1} r_i(t)] [f_1(t) - E_{t-1} f_1(t)] \\
&= E_{t-1} (u_t^i \epsilon_t) \\
Cov_{t-1} (r_i(t), f_2(t)) &= E_{t-1} [r_i(t) - E_{t-1} r_i(t)] [f_2(t) - E_{t-1} f_2(t)] \\
&= E_{t-1} (u_t^i \omega_t) \\
Var_{t-1} (f_1(t)) &= E_{t-1} [f_1(t) - E_{t-1} f_1(t)]^2 \\
&= E_{t-1} \epsilon_t^2 \\
Var_{t-1} (f_2(t)) &= E_{t-1} [f_2(t) - E_{t-1} f_2(t)]^2 \\
&= E_{t-1} \omega_t^2.
\end{aligned}
$$

Decomposing the sequences, $(\omega_t u_t^i)$, (ω_t^2), $(\epsilon_t u_t^i)$, and (ϵ_t^2) into their forecastable and unforecastable components, one has,

$$r_i(t) = \frac{E_{t-1} (\epsilon_t u_t^i)}{E_{t-1} (\epsilon_t^2)} E_{t-1} (f_1(t)) + \frac{E_{t-1} (\omega_t u_t^i)}{E_{t-1} (\omega_t^2)} E_{t-1} (f_2(t)) + u_t^i$$

$$i=1, ..., n, \qquad (3.2.5)$$

where
$$f_1(t) = E_{t-1} (f_1(t)) + \epsilon_t \qquad (3.2.6)$$
$$f_2(t) = E_{t-1} (f_2(t)) + \omega_t \qquad (3.2.7)$$
$$\epsilon_t u_i(t) = E_{t-1} (\epsilon_t u_i(t)) + v_t^i \qquad (3.2.8)$$
$$\omega_t u_i(t) = E_{t-1} (\omega_t u_i(t)) + \delta_t^i \quad i=1, ..., n \qquad (3.2.9)$$
$$\epsilon_t^2 = E_{t-1} (\epsilon_t^2) + v_t \qquad (3.2.10)$$
$$\omega_t^2 = E_{t-1} (\omega_t^2) + z_t , \qquad (3.2.11)$$

where v_t^i, δ_t^i, v_t, and z_t are the unforecastable components of $\epsilon_t u_t^i, \omega_t u_t^i$, ϵ_t^2, and ω_t^2, respectively.

The above system can be estimated either by (1) Maximum Likelihood Estimation (MLE) with a distribution assumption about the error structure or (2) Hansen's [1982] Generalized Method Moments (GMM) which does not need the assumption about the error distribution. The GMM is chosen for estimation in this paper because of its robustness in error distributions and its parsimony in parameters.

Using Hansen's [1982] GMM and assuming autoregressions of $\epsilon_t u_t^i$, ϵ_t^2, $\omega_t u_t^i$, and ω_t^2, the time-varying betas can be estimated.

Denote the q-dimensional parameter vector of interest by β, its true value by β_0, and the system's p-dimensional innovation vector by,

$$\omega_t \, (\beta_0) \;=\; (u_t^1 \, (\beta_0), \; v_t^1 \, (\beta_0), \; \delta_t^1 \, (\beta_0), \; ...,$$
$$u_t^n \, (\beta_0), \; v_t^n \, (\beta_0), \; \delta_t^n \, (\beta_0), \; \epsilon_t \, (\beta_0), \; \omega_t \, (\beta_0), \; v_t \, (\beta_0), \; z_t \, (\beta_0))'$$

Let $z_{t-1} \, (\beta_0)$ be an m-dimensional vector of date t-1 information, uncorrelated to $\omega_t \, (\beta_0)$, to serve as instrumental variables. Since $\omega_t \, (\beta_0)$ has the interpretation of being a vector of prediction errors, it implies a family of orthogonality conditions, $E(w_t \, (\beta_0) \otimes z_{t-1} \, (\beta_0)) = 0$. The GMM estimator of β_0, b_T, minimizes the quadratic criterion function,

$$\phi \, (\beta) \;=\; [(1/T) \sum_t^T (\omega_t \, (\beta) \otimes z_{t-1} \, (\beta))]' \; (S_T)^{-1}$$
$$\text{x} \; [(1/T) \sum_t^T (\omega_t \, (\beta) \otimes z_{t-1} \, (\beta))] \, , \qquad (3.2.12)$$

where,

$$S_T \;=\; (1/T) \sum_t^T (\omega_t \, (b) \, \omega_t \, (b)' \otimes z_{t-1} \, (b) \, z_{t-1} \, (b)') \, ,$$

and b is a consistent estimator of β_0. Asymptotically, $\sqrt{T} \, (b_T - \beta_0)$ is normally distributed with mean zero and covariance matrix,

$$\Omega \;=\; (D' \, S^{-1} \, D)^{-1} \, , \qquad (3.2.13)$$

where $D \;=\; E \, [\partial \, (\omega_t \, (\beta_0) \otimes z_{t-1} \, (\beta_0)) \, / \, \partial\beta'] \, ,$

and $S = E [\omega_t (\beta_0) \omega_t (\beta_0)' \otimes z_{t-1} (\beta_0) z_{t-1} (\beta_0)']$

is the spectral density matrix of $(\omega_t (\beta_0) \otimes z_{t-1} (\beta_0))$ at frequency 0.

The following sample estimates, D_T and S_T, consistently estimate matrices D and S.

$$D_T = (1/T) \sum_1^T [\partial (\omega_t (b_T) \otimes z_{t-1} (b_T) / \partial \beta'] ,$$

and

S_T as defined above.

This choice of the weighting matrix, S_T, yields a heteroskedasticity-consistent estimate of the covariance matrix of b_T.

Since $\omega_t(\beta)$ depends on past $\omega(\beta)$'s, the derivatives of $\omega_t(\beta)$ with respect to the parameter vector, β, will involve derivatives of $\omega_{t-1}(\beta)$, $\omega_{t-2}(\beta)$, ... The recursive structure will make the analytical derivatives difficult to get. The numerical derivatives are used instead to minimize $\phi(\beta)$ and to calculate the standard errors according to Equation 3.2.13. Princeton University's GQOPT package will be used for this estimation. The initial values of $\omega_t(\beta)$ (i.e., observations prior to the sample period) are set to their theoretical values of zero under the null hypothesis. A two-step procedure is used in estimation. An initial value of β, used to construct the weighting matrix, S_T, is obtained by performing autoregression of the variables involved in Equations 3.2.5 through 3.2.11. Final estimates are obtained by repeating the minimization of Equation 3.2.13 using the first-step estimates in the construction of the weighting matrix, S_T.

The above econometric specification represents a joint hypothesis that includes the two-factor model as an appropriate model in explaining the sample deposit-institution stock returns, a particular information set, specifications for conditional expectations, rational expectations, and the appropriateness of the sample data. Hansen's specification test can be used to test this joint hypothesis. The minimized values of the quadratic form in Equation 3.2.12 are distributed under the null hypothesis with degrees of freedom equal to the number of orthogonality conditions minus the number of parameters estimated. This statistic provides a test of the overidentifying restrictions. Consistent estimates of the parameters could be obtained with the number of orthogonality conditions equal to the number of parameters. When the number of orthogonality conditions exceeds the number of parameters, the model is overidentified. A test of specification is employed to estimate the parameters with an exactly identified model, and then those parameters are used to see if the expectation of the product of the error term and the extra instruments is small (see Hansen [1982]).

SECTION 3.3
THE SAMPLE DATA

The sample is constructed from data tapes prepared by the Center for Research in Security Prices (CRSP) at the University of Chicago. All commercial banks and S&L's are selected for which the CRSP tape shows monthly returns from June, 1976 to December, 1987. To allow me to compare my result with that of Kane and Unal [1988], my sample is an extension of theirs, including the years 1986 and 1987. The other reason for choosing this sample period is that deposit institutions faced dramatic changes in monetary policies, deregulations, and third-world debt problems. It is interesting to study the risks and their variability for deposit institutions during the sample period. Table 1 in Chapter II lists these large banks and S&L's and gives their asset sizes. Monthly data is chosen because most economic data are collected and compiled in monthly intervals. To test for possible intraindustry differences, banks are further classified into two categories (which form two portfolios): a class of "money-center banks" is determined from Citicorp's competitor list (Sinkey, 1986, p. 249), and other banks are classified into "regional banks." The third portfolio includes several big S&L's.

The risk-free rate is proxied by the return to a one-month treasury bill. The CRSP equally-weighted NYSE return is used as the market proxy. The holding-period return on the long-term government bond is used as a proxy for the return to the interest rate factor. Following are the reasons for utilizing the interest rate index. First, Merton [1973] suggests that the long-term government bond can be thought of as a hedging portfolio for the risk of changing the interest rate. It is also almost uncorrelated with the market index--the sample correlation is 0.07--which justifies the use of the two-factor model discussed in Section 3.2. Second, Unal and Kane (1987) find that bank and S&L stock returns are sensitive only to the holding period return of long-term government bonds; they are not sensitive to short-term government bills. The return on the long-term government bond is obtained from Ibbotson Associates [1988].

Table 6 reports the time-series means, the standard deviations, and the first six autocorrelations of the data. The mean return of the equally-weighted CRSP portfolio is 1.18%. The mean return of the interest rate index is 0.8%, and it shows a first-order correlation of 0.06. The standard deviation of the interest rate index is large relative to its mean, suggesting the higher volatility of the interest rate over the sample period. Furthermore, the third-order autocorrelation is a rather large number, -0.19, suggesting the higher autocorrelations of the data. The three deposit-institution stock portfolios have similar mean returns and standard deviations. The first-order correlation is not small. The high autocorrelations suggest the appropriateness of the autoregressive form for the variables in the model.

SECTION 3.4
EMPIRICAL SPECIFICATION AND RESULTS

For estimation, the conditional expectations appearing in Equations 3.2.5 through 3.2.11 have to be parameterized, but the theory does not tell us the exact functional form of the

Table 6

Time-series means, standard deviations, and autocorrelations of the returns
of the deposit-institution stock portfolios from June, 1976 to December, 1987

	Market Index and Interest Rate Index		Three Deposit-institution Portfolios		
	EM	Int.	RP1	RP2	RP3
Mean	0.0118	0.0085	0.0111	0.0113	0.0165
Std. dev.	0.0470	0.0373	0.0694	0.0723	0.0567
Auto- 1:	0.03	0.06	0.17	0.19	0.16
correlation 2:	-0.09	-0.01	0.01	0.02	-0.16
at lag 3:	-0.05	-0.19	-0.13	-0.07	-0.06
4:	-0.04	0.02	-0.04	0.01	-0.07
5:	0.18	0.08	0.08	0.03	0.19
6:	-0.07	0.09	-0.14	-0.04	-0.11

EM is the CRSP equally-weighted index of equity returns listed on the New York Stock
Exchange. Int. is the interest rate index proxied by the holding-period return in the long-term
government bond from Ibbotson Associates [1988]. RP1, RP2, and RP3 are the portfolio
returns for the sample "money center" banks, regional banks, and S&L's.

conditional expectations. Harvey's [1988] work suggests that we might be able to use macroeconomic variables as the condition set. However, the empirical specifications--using the four macroeconomic variables noted in Chapter II--are rejected by Hansen's specification test (see details in Appendix E), suggesting that it may not be a feasible direction. The following specification of the systems in Equations 3.2.5 through 3.2.11 assumes the autoregressions for the conditional mean, conditional variance, and covariance. In order to simplify the computation, a strong effort is made to keep the model parsimonious. Allowing more lags in the model will permit us to capture more "memory" of the time-series data. However, when more lags are allowed in the specification, more parameters are introduced and need to be estimated, which makes the estimation more complex and time-consuming. To compromise, an AR(3) is specified for the model.

$$r_i(t) = \frac{E_{t-1}(\epsilon_t u_t^i)}{E_{t-1}(\epsilon_t^2)} E_{t-1}(f_1(t)) + \frac{E_{t-1}(\omega_t u_t^i)}{E_{t-1}(\omega_t^2)} E_{t-1}(f_2(t)) + u_t^i,$$
$$i = 1, 2, 3,$$

$$f_1(t) = E_{t-1}(f_1(t)) + \epsilon_t = \alpha_0 + \sum_{j=1}^{3} \alpha_j f_j(t-j) + \epsilon_t,$$

$$f_2(t) = E_{t-1}(f_2(t)) + \omega_t = \beta_0 + \sum_{j=1}^{3} \beta_j f_j(t-j) + \omega_t,$$

$$\epsilon_t u_t^i = E_{t-1}(\epsilon_t u_t^i) + v_t^i = \alpha_0^i + \sum_{j=1}^{3} \alpha_j^i \epsilon_{t-j} u_{t-j}^i + v_t^i,$$
$$i = 1, 2, 3,$$

$$\omega_t u_t^i = E_{t-1}(\omega_t u_t^i) + \delta_t^i = \beta_0^i + \sum_{j=1}^{3} \beta_i^i \omega_{t-j} u_t^i + \delta_t^i,$$
$$i = 1, 2, 3,$$

$$\epsilon_t^2 = E_{t-1}(\epsilon_t^2) + v_t = \gamma_0 + \sum_{j=1}^{3} \gamma_j \epsilon_{t-j}^2 + v_t,$$

$$\omega_t^2 = E_{t-1}(\omega_t^2) + z_t = 1_0 + \sum_{j=1}^{3} 1_j \omega_{t-j}^2 + z_t.$$

The above autoregressive specification follows the idea of the ARCH modeling strategy (see Engel [1982]) where the conditional covariance and the conditional variance are modeled as functions of their past values.

The instrument set is kept small for the same reason Mark [1988, p. 345] considered. The constant, lagged market returns, the bond return, and previous forecast errors for the system are believed to be good instruments, in the sense that the estimation is more stable. These instruments generate a family of fifty-two orthogonality conditions. The number of parameters is forty, and the number of equations in the above system is thirteen. The results are reported in Table 7.

The test of the overidntifying restrictions--given by the chi-square statistic with twelve degrees of freedom--does not rejct the model at standard significance levels. The chi-square statistic is 12.12 with a p-value of 0.45. Many parameters are estimated with precision. The signifcance of the parameters of the conditional variance and the conditional covariance (the γ_i's and 1_i's and the α_i's and β_i's) implies a significant time-variation of covariances and variances of the deposit-institution stock returns.

In order to investigate the time-variation of the betas, a Wald test of a constant-beta version of the model that sets $\gamma_j = 1_j = \alpha_j^i = \beta_j^i = 0$, where i = 1, 2, 3 and j = 1, 2, 3, is performed. Under the null hypothesis, the betas are constant and the Wald test statistic is distributed as a chi-square with 24 degrees of freedom. The results are reported in Table 7. The null hypothesis can be rejected at better than the 1% level. However, rejection of the Wald test does not necessarily lead to the conclusion that the betas are time-varying, since it is possible that both conditional variance and conditional covariance change proportionally.

Table 7

Generalized method-of-moments estimates of the two-factor ARCH model for three deposit-institution stock portfolios, with market index and interest rate index as the two factors. Test of the model's overidentifying restrictions and the Wald test of constant betas. (The asymptotic t-ratios are in parentheses.)

Market Parameters

	$\alpha 0$	$\alpha 1$	$\alpha 2$	$\alpha 3$
Conditional Mean	0.0027 (0.03)	0.0885 (1.01)	-0.4681* (5.34)	-0.5516* (6.28)
	$\gamma 0$	$\gamma 1$	$\gamma 2$	$\gamma 3$
Conditional Variance	0.0011 (0.01)	0.0183 (0.20)	0.0165 (0.18)	0.1877* (2.14)

Interest Rate Parameters

	$\beta 0$	$\beta 1$	$\beta 2$	$\beta 3$
Conditional Mean	0.0026 (0.03)	0.2856* (3.26)	-0.2243* (2.56)	-0.2073* (2.36)
	10	11	12	13
Conditional Variance	0.1188 (1.35)	0.7869* (8.97)	0.2039* (2.33)	0.5552* (6.32)

Table 7 (cont.)

Conditional Covariance Parameters

Deposit-Institution Stock Portfolios

Covariance with Market

	RP1	RP2	RP3
	α_0^1 0.0011 (0.01)	α_0^2 0.0002 (0.00)	α_0^3 0.0014 (0.02)
	α_1^1 0.7436* (8.48)	α_1^2 0.3273* (3.73)	α_1^3 0.1083 (1.23)
	α_2^1 0.4837* (5.52)	α_2^2 0.3334* (3.80)	α_2^3 0.2417* (2.76)
	α_3^1 -0.2134* (2.43)	α_3^2 -0.1221 (1.39)	α_3^3 -0.2709* (3.08)

Table 7 (cont.)

Deposit-Institution Stock Portfolios (cont.)

Covariance with Interest Rate

β_0^1 0.0029 (0.03)	β_0^2 0.0030 (0.03)	β_0^3 0.0025 (0.03)
β_1^1 0.4573* (5.21)	β_1^2 0.3224* (3.67)	β_1^3 0.1785* (2.03)
β_2^1 0.3990* (4.54)	β_2^2 0.3299* (3.76)	β_2^3 0.1439 (1.64)
β_3^1 -0.8919* (10.17)	β_3^2 -0.7506* (8.55)	β_3^3 -0.2037* (2.32)

Table 7 (cont.)

Test of Overidentifying Restrictions	Wald Test of Constant Betas
$\chi^2 (12) = 12.12$	$\chi^2 (24) = 102.09$
p-value $= 0.45$	p-value $= 0.00$

a. The test of the overidentifying restrictions is implied by the model reported here. Test statistic is distributed as $\chi^2 (12)$.

b. The test of the restrictions, $\gamma_j = 1_j = \alpha_j^i = \beta_j^i = 0$, where i, j = 1, 2, 3, is implied by a constant beta specification. The test statistic is distributed as $\chi^2 (24)$.

c. RP1, RP2, and RP3 represent the three deposit-institution stock portfolios.

d. An * means that the coefficient is statistically significant at 5%.

SECTION 3.5
DISCUSSION OF THE EMPIRICAL RESULTS

Some qualitative results may be obtained from plotting the market betas and the interest rate betas estimated from the model against time. Figures 4-6 plot the time-varying market betas for the three deposit-institution stock portfolios, with the CRSP equally-weighted return as the market index. All three pictures seem to show that market risk varies significantly during the sample period. The constant market risks from the constant-beta version of the two-factor model are also plotted; they are 0.94, 0.89, and 0.80 for the money-center banks, the regional banks, and the S&L's, respectively. The constant market betas do not show a significant difference. One reason for this is because all the deposit institutions in the sample are very large institutions and presumably, therefore, are equally efficient in hedging risks.

Figure 4 shows the change in market risk for the money-center banks for the sample period. Market risk ranges from 0.02 to 1.50 and changes greatly during this period. The end of 1979 shows a small increase in market risk, but it is followed by a big drop in market risk in the early 1980's. This may be the net result of many events which occurred during that period, a partial list of which includes a change in the Fed's operating procedures, the DIDMCA of 1980, and the modification of insolvency rules by the FSLIC. Among these, the DIDMCA reduced the absolute amount of non-interest-bearing reserves that banks have to hold, and they eliminated the interest rate differentials on the time deposit between banks and S&L's. This increased protection for banks should decrease their market risks, as suggested by Peltzman's [1976] theory of regulation.[2] The end of 1982 to early 1983, the end of 1984 to early 1985, and the middle of 1986 seem to be the periods when market risk increased to a large extent. There is some evidence that the market risk after 1982 was higher and more volatile.

Figure 5 portrays the change in the market risk of the regional banks, where market risk changes from 0.4 to 1.7.

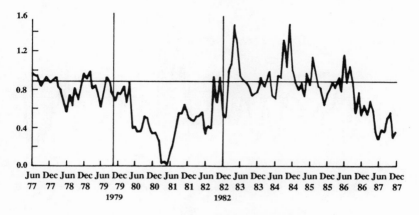

Figure 4. Market Risk for Money-Center Banks, 1977-87

————— constant Beta = .89

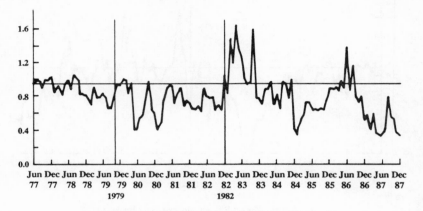

Figure 5. Market Risk for Regional Banks, 1977-87

————— constant Beta = .94

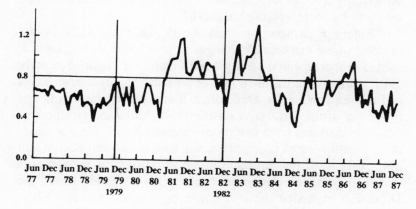

Figure 6. Market Risk for S &L's, 1977-87

————— constant Beta = .80

Probably for the same reasons as the money-center banks, the level of market risk was lower during the period from 1979-1982. From late 1982 to early 1983 and the end of 1986 appear to be the periods of high market risk, while the end of 1979 shows only a small increase in market risk. Again, market risk seems to be more volatile after 1982.

Figure 6 depicts the market risk for the S&L's of the sample, where market risk changes from 0.3 to 1.4. Market risk started to increase in the early 1980's and, then, jumped in early 1981, which is earlier than that of both the money-center banks and the regional banks. One potential explanation for this is that the effect of the DIDMCA on the profitability and riskiness of S&L's is different from that on commercial banks. On one hand, the uniform reserve requirement for both banks and S&L's and deregulations of interest rate ceilings eliminated two advantages that S&L's have relative to banks. On the other hand, the DIDMCA expanded the investment opportunity set of S&L's. The middle of 1981 and the end of 1982 to early 1983 both show an increased market risk.

In general, the results are consistent with the findings of Kane and Unal [1988] which demonstrate that deposit-institution stocks showed very volatile market risks in the 1980's. In particular, the big increase in market risks for both banks and S&L's at the end of 1982 suggests that there may be regime changes--switches--when one applies the switching regression methods to the sample. However, the pattern of an increase in market risks and, then, a decrease is not captured by the switching regression model of Kane and Unal [1988]. Another interesting point to note is that all three groups of deposit institutions show increases in market risks at the middle of 1986 and decreases afterwards, which is not discussed in the study of Kane and Unal [1987] because their sample ends at the year 1985.

Figures 7-9 plot the time-series pattern of the risks of the second factor: the interest rate factor. The CRSP equally-weighted return is chosen as the market proxy. All interest rate

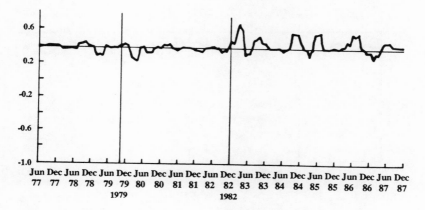

Figure 7. Interest Rate Risk for Money-Center Banks, 1977-87

————— constant Beta = .39

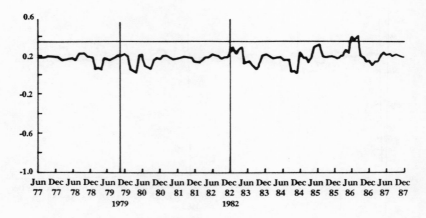

Figure 8. Interest Rate Risk for Regional Banks, 1977-87

——————— constant Beta = .35

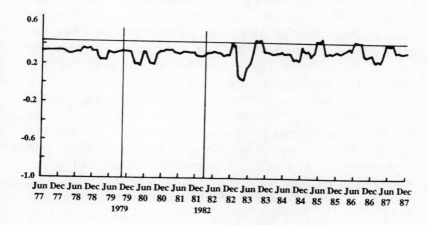

Figure 9. Interest Rate Risk for S &L's, 1977-87

——— constant Beta = .43

risks are positive, which is expected since the holding period returns on bonds are negatively correlated with changes in the level of the interest rates. A positive value of interest rate risk means that the firm's market value declines when interest rates rise. This is because the assets of deposit institutions generally take longer to mature than do their liabilities; the value of their assets is more sensitive to changes in the interest rates than the value of their liabilities. As a result, when interest rates rise, the net worth of a deposit institution's assets falls more than the value of its liabilities. The constant interest rate risks from the constant-beta version of the two-factor model are 0.39, 0.35, and 0.43 for the money-center banks, the regional banks, and the S&L's, respectively. As in the case of the market risks, they do not show a significant difference. All pictures show that the interest rate risks are not as volatile as the market risks. For bank stocks, these results are consistent with the findings of Kane and Unal [1988] which show that little significant temporal variation occurs in bank interest rate sensitivity during the years 1975-1985. This suggests that the large deposit institutions were probably able to measure and control the interest rate risk at an appropriate level. In particular, my study shows that the patterns of the change in interest rate risk remain the same throughout the regime changes of the Fed's monetary policy changes in 1979 and 1982. This suggests that banks may have adjusted to the volatility of interest rates by designing financial hedges, like interest rate futures and swaps. At the end of 1982, all three types of deposit institutions showed a small increase in interest rate risk, indicating that the deregulations may allow the deposit institutions to take a more unbalanced position. Because the results suggest that both bank and S&L stock returns have a higher and more volatile interest rate beta since 1982, evidence different from the findings of Kane and Unal [1988]--that bank stock returns were interest-sensitive primarily during the 1979-1982 era, but S&L stock returns were interest-sensitive during the period 1975-1985--is provided.

The market risks and interest rate risks for the deposit institutions show only small increases at the end of 1979. This is consistent with the evidence found by Aharony, Saunders, and Swary [1986] that no significant change occurred for banks and S&L's in either market or interest rate risk around October, 1979. However, the fact that both market risk and interest rate risk changed near the end of 1982 deserves some explanation.

Many significant events occurred during the latter half of 1982: in August of that year, Mexico declared a moratorium on its foreign debt; in November, Congress passed the Garn-St. Germain Act which, among other purposes, authorized Money Market Deposit Accounts and SuperNow Accounts; and in December, 1982, the effective lift of Regulation Q by the Depository Institutions Deregulation Committee--established under the DIDMCA--took place. In 1982, the number of failed and problem institutions increased sharply (see Kane and Unal [1988]). Because deposit-institution stock returns reflect all relevant information affecting profits and risks of deposit institutions, an increase in market risks and interest rate risks indicates that the risk exposure of these deposit institutions to the changing environment has increased.

Figures 10-12 depict both the expected excess returns, i.e., the total risk premiums, and the actual excess returns of the three groups of deposit institutions. Most of the expected returns portrayed are positive and below 1.0%. They change over time and closely trace the variations of the actual excess returns.

The discussion which follows compares the results found in this study with those observed in previous studies. The existing empirical findings in the banking literature on the two-index model, with market and interest rate indexes, is far from analogous. It has been shown that the market beta and the interest rate beta can be quite different, with different proxies, time periods, or number of institutions used in research (see Unal and Kane [1987]). In order to make a comparison with previous studies performed, Table 8 reports the estimates of market and interest rate betas found by different authors. As

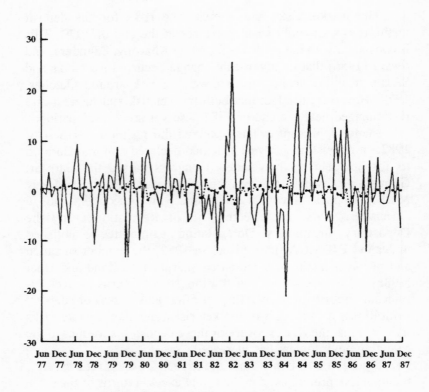

Figure 10. The Expected and Actual Stock Returns for
Money-Center Banks.

———— The Actual return
***** The Expected return

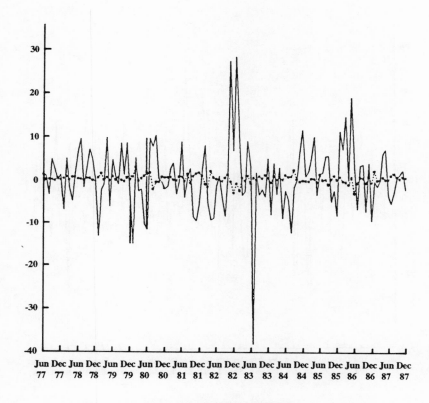

Figure 11. The Expected and Actual Stock Returns for
Regional Banks.

——— The Actual return
★★★★★ The Expected return

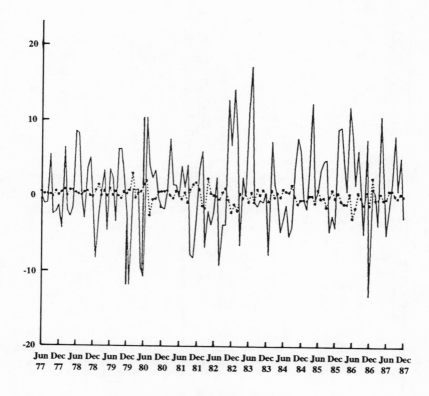

Figure 12. The Expected and Actual Stock Returns for
S.&L.s.

———— The Actual return
***** The Expected return

Table 8

Literature estimates of market and interest rate betas for deposit institutions and their comparison to the results found in this study

	β_m	β_i	Analysis Period	Observations	# of Banks
1. FJ	0.56 (18.5)	0.13 (3.5)	1/76 - 11/81	weekly	68
2. SP	0.67 (8.15)	-0.40 (-4.41)	1/77 - 12/84	monthly	78
3. KU	0.75 (8.10)	0.35 (3.48)	1/77 - 12/84	monthly	31
4. BL	0.53 (80.83)	-0.02 (-6.71)	1/78 - 6/84	daily	44
5. FS	0.88 (13.98)	0.50 (5.63)	4/76 - 12/87	monthly	33

1. Flannery and James, 1984, use the NYSE Composite Index as the market return. The interest rate beta is estimated using the residuals of an AR(3) model for the weekly holding-period return for GNMA eight percent certificates.

2. Scott and Peterson, 1986, use the S&P 500 return index and monthly percentage changes in 30-year treasury bond yields as proxies for the market index and the interest rate index, respectively.

3. Kane and Unal, 1988, use value-weighted NYSE and AMEX stock indexes adjusted for dividends as the market proxy, and the monthly holding-period return on long-term government bonds is used as the interest rate proxy.

4. Brewer and Lee, 1986, use the value-weighted NYSE and AMEX composited index obtained from the CRSP to proxy market returns. Their proxy for the interest rate index is the difference between the three-month treasury bill rate at time t and the forward three-month treasury bill rate imbedded in the yield curve at time t-1. The reported estimates are obtained from cross-section time-series data.

5. My study of the constant-beta model uses an equally-weighted NYSE stock index adjusted for dividends as the market proxy, and the monthly holding-period return on long-term government bonds is used as the interest rate proxy.

shown, all studies suggest that deposit-institution stocks show a market beta considerably lower than unity. This is consistent with the belief that the market risk of deposit institutions is below the average. The interest rate beta varies from positive to negative in different studies, which may result from the fact that different interest rate indexes are used. For example, long-term bond prices respond more to a given change in the level of interest rates than do short-term bond prices.

The following discussion also compares the market betas and interest rate betas calculated from the two-factor ARCH model to those of the constant-beta version of the two-index model and, then, to those of the switching regression betas from Kane and Unal [1988]. Figures 4-9 also depict both constant betas and time-varying betas. The three constant market betas are approximately the same as the average of the time-varying market betas, while the constant interest rate betas tend to be a bit higher than the average of the time-varying interest rate betas.

Another comparison made is with that of the switching regression model. Figures 13-16 depict the betas from the switching regression estimation done by Kane and Unal [1988], the constant-beta version of the two-index model, and the time-varying betas from my two-factor ARCH models. From Table 9, one can see that the money-center banks have two switching points from 1977-1985, one occurring in December, 1979, and the other, in March, 1982. Before the first switch, the market beta is 1.03; between the first and second switches, the market beta is 0.07; following the second switch, the market beta becomes 1.35.

It can be seen from Figure 13 that for the first period, i.e., before the first switching point, the market beta from the switching regression model is higher than both the constant beta and the time-varying beta. In the second period, i.e., after the first switch and before the second one, the beta from the switching regression model is much lower than the constant beta and the time-varying beta. In the last period after the second

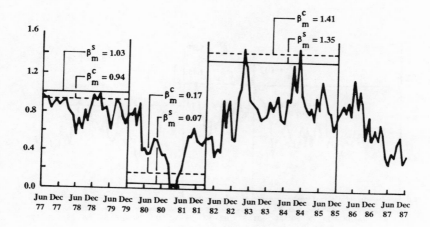

Figure 13. Market Risk for Money-Center Banks, 1977-87.

—————— Switching Regression Beta from Kane and Unal (1988), β_m^s

- - - - - - Constant Beta during the Switching Period, β_m^c

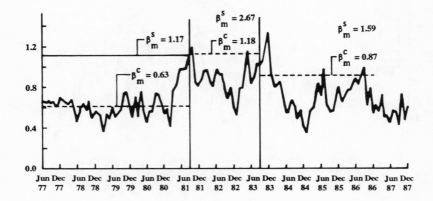

Figure 14. Market Risk for S &L's, 1977-87.

——————— Switching Regression Beta from Kane and Unal (1988), β_m^s

- - - - - - Constant Beta during the Switching Period, β_m^c

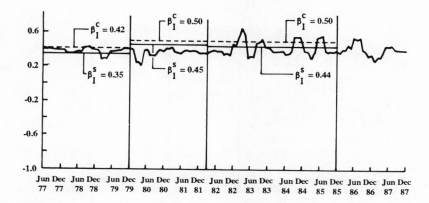

Figure 15. Interest Rate Risk for Money-Center Banks, 1977-87.

————— Switching Regression Beta from Kane and Unal (1988), β_I^s

– – – – – Constant Beta during the Switching Period, β_I^c

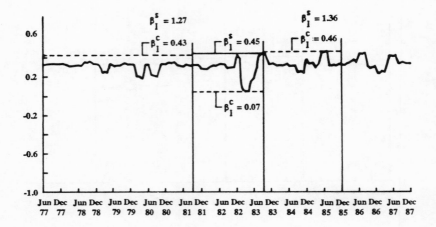

Figure 16. Interest Rate Risk for S &L's, 1977-87.

——— Switching Regression Beta from Kane and Unal (1988), β_1^s

- - - - - Constant Beta during the Switching Period, β_1^c

Table 9[a]

Maximum-likelihood estimates of regime parameters for the years 1975-1985

Parameter	Money-Center Banks	Super-regional Banks	Regional Banks	S&L's
Starting date	1/75	1/75	1/75	1/75
β_{m1}	1.40*	1.36*	1.33*	1.84*
β_{i1}	.20	.33	.43	1.35
σ_1	.06	.04	.05	.09
Switch point	25.20	24.75	13.76	14.00
	(.98)	(.42)	(.42)	(.03)
Implied date	1/77	1/77	2/76	2/76
Switch std. dev.	.65	.12	.25	.01
β_{m2}	1.03*	.92*	.43*	-1.12*
β_{i2}	.35	-.26	.35	3.02*
σ_2	.02	.02	.02	.03
Switch point	60.43	53.19	45.19	28.15
	(3.11)	(1.47)	(5.93)	(.9)
Implied date	12/79	5/79	9/78	4/77
Switch std. dev.	1.21	.15	7.00	1.17

Table 9 (cont.)

β_{m3}	.07	.45*	.57*	1.17*
β_{i3}	.45*	.54*	.27*	1.27*
σ_3	.04	.04	.04	.05
Switch point	86.53	81.62	95.34	81.30
	(6.28)	(4.98)	(8.22)	(.9)
Implied date	3/82	10/81	11/82	9/81
Switch std. dev.	2.1	2.8	.06	.1
β_{m4}	1.35*	1.19*	1.03*	2.67*
β_{i4}	.44	.16	.38	.43
σ_4	.06	.04	.03	.10
Switch point	---	118.12	---	105.30
		(.1)		(9.1)
Implied date	---	10/84	---	9/83
Switch std. dev.	---	.59	---	1.59
β_{m5}	---	1.37*	---	1.10*
β_{i5}	---	-.24	---	1.36*
σ_5	---	.01	---	.06
Ending date	12/85	12/85	12/85	12/85

[a] This table is taken from Table 1 of Kane and Unal [1988].

switching point, both the constant beta and the market beta from the switching regression model are higher than the time-varying beta. Overall, the two-factor ARCH model does capture the pattern of changing market risk for the money-center banks.

Figure 14 illustrates the comparison of the market betas for the sample S&L's. The market betas from the switching regression method for the three periods represented are 1.17, 2.67, and 1.59, respectively. All of them are much higher than both the constant betas and the time-varying betas in the corresponding periods. In addition, the time-varying betas are much closer to the constant betas in the corresponding periods. An illustration of the comparison between the regional banks in this study with those of Kane and Unal [1987] cannot be drawn because the sample of regional banks used here pools both samples of Kane and Unal's super-regional and regional banks.

Figures 15 and 16 show comparisons of the interest rate betas from the switching regression model with the time-varying interest rate betas for money-center banks and S&L's. Figure 15 shows that for the money-center banks, the interest rate betas from the switching regression model, the constant-beta model, and my two-factor ARCH model are all very close. However, the interest rate betas from the switching regression model for the S&L's tend to be much higher than those of the constant betas and the time-varying betas in Figure 16. The tendency to observe higher market betas and interest rate betas from the switching regression model compared to those of the time-varying betas seen from the two-factor ARCH models needs further analysis. However, it is interesting to compare studies of both the switching regression model and my two-factor ARCH model with those of the constant version of the two-index market models. It seems clear from Figures 13-16 that the betas calculated from the two-factor ARCH model are more similar to the betas of the constant-beta version of the two-index model than to those of the switching regression model.

SECTION 3.6
CONCLUSIONS AND FURTHER
RESEARCH PLANS

This study takes the ARCH approach to a two-factor model for deposit-institution stock returns. Risks of deposit institutions are specified within the framework of Merton's multi-factor asset pricing model, and the ARCH modeling strategy is then applied to deposit-institution stock returns in order to study the time-varying market and interest rate risks. For the sample deposit institutions, it was found that both market risks and interest rate risks changed during the period 1977-1987. The market risks have been higher and more volatile since 1982, and the interest rate risks have been less volatile than the market risks. There is evidence of increasing interest rate risks at the end of 1982. Contrary to popular belief, the interest rate risks for the sample deposit institutions do not respond in a significant way to regime changes in the Fed's monetary policy (1979, 1982). Model specification tests suggest the usefulness of the two-factor ARCH models in studying deposit-institution stock returns.

The major contribution of this study is that it provides a method for studying the time-varying risks of deposit institutions. The two-factor ARCH model can be used to measure the changing pattern of risks of any deposit institution. The information learned from applying the two-factor ARCH model to deposit-institution stock returns may help regulators design risk-related deposit insurance. It may also prove helpful to deposit-institution managers as they innovate new financial hedges against identified risks.

Other risk factors for the deposit-institution industry can be identified, and they then can be analyzed in the framework of a multi-factor model. The effects of a change in specific regulations or monetary policies on the ARCH models specified in this study for deposit-institution stock returns can also be examined. The market and interest rate risks of deposit institutions can be related to balance sheet data--for example, the capital/asset ratio--of the institutions. These works are left for further studies.

Endnotes

1. As argued by Ingersoll [1987], this case is not as special as it may seem because we are free to choose the residual version of the state variable (after "regressing" the original state variable on the market) as the state variable. In the empirical analysis which follows, the sample correlation of the equally-weighted market return and the long-term government bond is 0.07, nearly uncorrelated.

2. Peltzman [1976] argues that regulation alters the riskiness of the affected firms. By insulating firms from demand and cost changes, regulation lowers the variability of earnings (and stock prices) from what they would have been otherwise. If the cost and demand changes are economy-wide--like the depression in the early 1980's--regulation should reduce the market risk of banks.

Chapter IV

The Changing Risks of Banks:
A Moving Regression Approach

SECTION 4.1
INTRODUCTION

The changing economic environment for the U.S. banking industry since the late 1970's poses a serious challenge to both regulators and managers. To protect their insurance fund and ensure proper risk-taking of banks, bank regulators are increasingly interested in measuring the risks of banks. Bank managers are also interested in risk measurement because of the need to design financial hedges against the increasing uncertainties facing banks.

One way to assess the risks of a bank is to examine the exposure of bank stock returns to the uncertainties of the macroeconomic variables in the economy. Previous studies--for example, Stone [1974], Lloyd and Shick [1977], Chance and Lane [1980], Lynge and Zumwalt [1980], Flannery and James [1984], Booth and Officer [1985], Scott and Peterson [1986], and Bae [1990]--try to identify the risks of deposit institutions by applying a two-index model consisting of a market index and an interest rate index. The coefficients of the model measure market risk (or market beta) and interest rate risk (or interest rate beta). Akella and Chen [1990] provide a survey of the studies on the interest rate sensitivity of bank stock returns. The consensus seems to be that, at least for some periods during the 1970's and 1980's, bank stocks were interest rate sensitive.

More recently, many researchers have turned their attention to the issue of changing market and interest rate risks. For example, Booth, Officer, and Henderson [1985] show that the market risk for commercial banks tends to increase over time, and during the period 1966-1986, it was positively correlated with interest rate levels. Kane and Unal [1988] investigate variability in the risk components of both bank and savings and loan stocks for the years 1975-1985. Using a switching regression method, they show that the market risk, interest rate risk, and residual risk of deposit-institution stock returns varied significantly during this period. Following Flannery and James [1984], Kwan [1991] develops and tests a random-coefficient model for commercial-bank stock returns, which controls for the time-varying interest rate beta caused by a bank's changing maturity structure. Kwan finds that interest rate changes on bank stock returns are positively related to the maturity mismatch between bank assets and liabilities. In contrast, Mitchell [1989] estimates bank exposure to interest rate risk and finds that during the period 1976-1983, bank total exposure to interest rate risk was quite small despite increased interest rate volatility and financial deregulation. Akella and Chen [1990] find evidence that the interest rate risk of banks has declined since 1980. Song [forthcoming] applies the Autoregressive Conditional Heteroscedastic (ARCH) modeling technique to the two-index model and finds that the market risks for his sample banks and S&L's were higher and more volatile during the 1980's than during the 1970's. The interest rate risk, however, was much more stable during the sample period 1976-1987.

Although there seems to be agreement that bank market risks changed greatly during the 1970's and 1980's, no clear consensus has emerged regarding the significance and variability of interest rate risks.[1] In addition, although there are some qualitative discussions about the causes of the changing risks--for example, deregulations and interest rate volatility factors--(see Kane and Unal [1988] and Song [forthcoming]) and some quantitative assessment of changing interest rate risk using the maturity structure of bank assets and liabilities (see Kwan [1991]), the literature simply ignores the issue of *quantitatively* measuring the changing risks due to changes in macroeconomic and financial variables.

This study employs a two-step approach to examine both the market and interest rate risks of a sample of commercial banks. In the first step, a moving-regression technique is applied to the two-index model for four bank portfolios. The moving betas obtained from the first step are then regressed on a set of macroeconomic and bank asset-composition variables. This approach is innovative in the following sense. First, the moving betas from the first step can identify to what extent the market and interest rate risks have been changed during the sample period. Second, the economic and financial variables that influence the risks of banks can be identified. Third, the data for bank stock returns cover more commercial banks than most previous studies. The goal here is to shed further light on the issue of changing risk exposures of commercial banks and to identify the macroeconomic and financial variables which affect these risks.

The results of this study show that both the market risk and the interest rate risk of banks have changed substantially over the years from 1973 to 1990. Also, it is found that several macroeconomic variables, such as long-term and short-term interest rates, the money supply, industrial production, and foreign-exchange rates, affect the market risks of banks. In addition, bank market risk is positively related to exposures to real estate loans. The effects of these macroeconomic and financial variables are somewhat different between the money-center banks and other banks.

SECTION 4.2
EMPIRICAL METHODOLOGY AND DATA

The methodology used in this study is a two-step approach. In the first step, the following two-index regressions are run:

$$R_{it} = \alpha_i + \beta_{im} R_{mt} + \beta_{iI} R_{It} + u_t,$$
$$t = 1, \ldots, T \text{ and } i = 1, \ldots, 4 \qquad (4.2.1)$$

where R_{it} is a monthly, equally-weighted bank holding company (BHC) portfolio return for portfolio i at time t; R_{mt} is the monthly, equally-weighted CRSP (i.e., Center for Research in Security Prices) NYSE/AMEX return index, including dividends; R_{it} is the interest rate index measured by the monthly holding-period returns of long-term U.S. government bonds obtained from Ibbotson Associates (1991)[2]; β_{im} and β_{iI} are the market beta and interest rate beta for portfolio i; and α_i is the intercept. The reasons for utilizing the interest rate index are the following. First, Merton [1973] suggests that the long-term government bond can be thought of as a hedging portfolio for the risk of changing the interest rate. Second, Unal and Kane [1987] find that bank and S&L stock returns are sensitive only to the holding-period returns of long-term bonds and not to yields on short-term treasury bills.

An alternative procedure which may be employed to estimate the market beta is to orthogonalize R_i against R_m and, then, to use the R_m index and the orthogonalized R_i index as the two indexes to approximate the market and interest rate betas. The interest rate beta can be estimated similarly by orthogonalizing the market index against the interest rate index. However, Giliberto [1985] shows that if Equation 4.2.1 describes the true return-generating process, then the orthogonalization of R_i against R_m will produce a biased estimate for the market beta. It will not affect the estimate for the interest rate beta, however, and vice versa. Because of the potential bias associated with the orthogonalized version of the model, both the market beta and the interest rate beta are estimated based on the unorthogonalized version of Equation 4.2.1.

Since BHC's and not individual banks are traded, the BHC's are used to investigate the changing market and interest rate risks of banks. Daily stock returns for the BHC's during the period 1973-1990 are obtained from the CRSP NYSE/AMEX and

NASDAQ files. This study begins with information from the year 1973 because the NASDAQ file carries return data only from the middle of 1972.

Because large banks may behave somewhat differently than smaller banks,[3] four equally-weighted BHC portfolios are formed, and monthly returns of those portfolios are calculated. The first portfolio, the Money-Center portfolio, consists of the nation's nine largest BHC's (see Appendix E, where the same classification that Kane and Unal [1988] used is applied). The second portfolio, the Stable portfolio, consists of 68 BHC's (again, see Appendix E). These 68 BHC's have complete return information available in the CRSP files from 1973 to 1990, and their stocks have been traded on the same exchange (either NYSE, AMEX, or NASDAQ) for the entire sample period. Because growing BHC's tend to be switched from the NASDAQ system to the organized exchanges, the Stable portfolio ensures that the empirical results are not dominated by BHC's that experienced extreme growth during the sample period. The third portfolio, the All portfolio, consists of 148 BHC's, the majority of which are carried by the Compustat Bank File. This portfolio contains BHC's that have been switched from the NASDAQ system to the organized exchange during the period from 1973 to 1990 as well as the BHC's that have not survived the whole sample period, hence avoiding the so-called survivorship bias.[4] The fourth portfolio, Moody's portfolio, consists of the 100 largest BHC's in terms of total assets at the end of the year 1990 (as reported in the 1991 edition of Moody's Banking and Finance Manual). These 100 BHC's are large companies, and many of them have experienced tremendous growth in the last two decades. In this sense, Moody's portfolio complements the Stable portfolio.[5]

The moving-regression coefficients for each of the four portfolios are estimated. During the sample period from January, 1973 to December, 1990, the first two-year's monthly data are used to obtain the market and interest rate betas in that two-year interval. To obtain the market beta and interest rate beta for the second two-year interval, the first observation is dropped and the twenty-fifth observation is added. This procedure is repeated until the end of the sample period. Employing this process, the market and interest rate betas for each two-year interval are obtained. The estimated market betas and interest rate betas (193 total observations) are referred to as the moving-market betas and the moving-interest rate betas, respectively. This approach is similar to Booth, Officer, and Henderson's [1985] study of the sensitivity of bank market risks to interest rates. In contrast to their strategy, however, this study applies the moving-regression technique to the two-index model. In addition, by relating the moving-market betas to macroeconomic and bank asset-composition variables, this study identifies why the risks have been changed.

In the second step, the moving-market betas are related to both the macroeconomic variables and the asset compositions of the commercial-banking industry. The selected variables for running the second-step regression are classified into three groups and are shown in Table 10. All of the time-series data are obtained from the *Citibase* data tape. The first group is related to the term structure of interest rates. Booth, Officer, and Henderson [1985] show that the market risk of banks is related to interest rate levels. Thistle, McLeod and Conrad [1989] find that the composition of the balance sheet depends on both the level and the change in interest rates. Since the market risks of banks are related to their balance-sheet compositions, they should also be related to interest rates. The slope of the term structure of interest rates may also influence bank profitability [Flannery, 1983]. For these reasons, the yield on a long-term U.S. government bond (LRATE) and the yield on a three-month treasury bill (SRATE) are chosen to represent the term structure of interest rates. An increase in long-term interest rates should reduce the risks of commercial banks, while an increase in short-term interest rates will increase bank risks.

Table 10
Macroeconomic variables and asset-composition variables

Group I: Term Structure of Interest Rates

    LRATE: Yield on long-term U.S. government bond.
    SRATE: Yield on three-month treasury bill.

Group II: General Business Climate

    M2:   Money supply (M2).
    IP: Industrial production index.
    ERATE: Index of weighted-average exchange value of U.S. dollar against currencies of other G-10 countries.

Group III: Asset Composition of the Commercial Banking Industry

    RLOAN: Ratio of commercial real estate loans held by commercial banks to total loans and securities of commercial banks.

    CLOAN: Ratio of commercial and industrial loans held by commercial banks to total loans and securities of commercial banks.

    GSEC: Ratio of governmental securities held by commercial banks to total loans and securities of commercial banks.

Source: Monthly data for the variables were either obtained directly from the *Citibase* data tapes or obtained indirectly from *Citibase* by calculating ratios.

The variables in the second group are indicators of the general business climate. There are many macroeconomic variables which measure business conditions. Some variables, like industrial production, money supply, the budget deficit, the unemployment rate, the trade balance, and exchange rates, affect general stock returns (Chen, Roll, and Ross [1986]; Abell and Krueger [1989]; Kim and Wu [1987]; and Hardouvelis [1987]). Money supply (M2) is chosen because banks produce money-related products. Hardouvelis [1987] finds that the stocks of financial companies (including banks) are most sensitive to monetary news. Abell and Krueger [1989] argue that banks, in general, are in a position to benefit directly from the creation of new money. Bank stock returns are amplified when the market advances under the conditions of an expanding money supply, which implies that bank betas tend to be positively associated with money supply.

The industrial production index (IP) is selected to represent the general business cycle. Chen, Roll, and Ross [1986] show that the same index can be used to measure the effect of real economic activity on stock returns. Because the performance of banks is quite sensitive to real economic activity, it is interesting to examine how changes in the real economy affect a bank's risk exposure. In a booming economy (as proxied by a rise in the IP), one would expect that as business default risks decrease, a bank's risk exposures would also decrease. The opposite may happen in the case of a recession.

An index of the weighted-average exchange value of the U.S. dollar against currencies of other G-7 countries (ERATE) captures the effect of international activities of banks on their risk exposures. Since the collapse of the Bretton Woods System in the early 1970's, exchange rates have been very volatile. During the sample period, the larger U.S. banks also substantially increased their international lending and currency business. Choi, Elyasiani and Kopecky [1992] find that bank stock returns are sensitive to an exchange-rate variable. However, the sensitivity depends on both the period of observation and the money-center status of banks. One would expect that the exchange-rate factor should affect betas of large banks--especially the money-center banks--because they have a large amount of international loans and engage substantially in foreign currency business. A stronger dollar may increase the default risks of international loans and depress the value of foreign currency holdings of large U.S. banks. Hence, one would anticipate that an increase in the exchange rate (an appreciation of the U.S. dollar) would result in higher market risks of large banks, especially for money-center banks.

The variables in the third group are asset-composition indicators for the commercial-banking industry. The first variable is the ratio of commercial real estate loans held by commercial banks to total loans and securities of commercial banks (RLOAN). The second variable is the ratio of commercial and industrial loans held by commercial banks to total loans and securities of commercial banks (CLOAN). The third variable is the ratio of government securities to total loans and securities of commercial banks (GSEC). Because different types of loans are associated with different levels of default risk and different maturity structures, the asset composition of the commercial-banking industry should relate to the riskiness of banks. The effects of these asset-composition variables on bank betas depend on the relative riskiness of these assets. For example, one expects that more government securities in a bank's portfolio are associated with a lower default risk. In contrast, riskier loans may generate a higher market risk.

Based on the above discussion, the second step of the regression model for the moving market risk is specified as follows:

$$
\begin{aligned}
MB_t = {} & \alpha_0 + \alpha_1 * LRATE_t + \alpha_2 * SRATE_t + \\
& \alpha_3 * M2_t + \alpha_4 * IP_t + \alpha_5 * ERATE_t + \\
& \alpha_6 * RLOAN_t + \alpha_7 * CLOAN_t + \alpha_8 * \\
& GSEC_t + u_t \qquad\qquad (4.2.2)
\end{aligned}
$$

where MB_t is the moving market beta at time t and u_t is the error term. The regressors are defined in Table 10. The expected signs are: $\alpha_1 > 0$, $\alpha_2 < 0$, $\alpha_3 > 0$, $\alpha_4 < 0$, $\alpha_5 > 0$, both α_6 and α_7 are uncertain, and $\alpha_8 < 0$.

Because the moving market betas are estimated using previous two-year information, they are the portfolio's market risk for the previous two years. Also, the selected macroeconomic variables are converted into two-year, moving-average series. For example, the LRATE is a two-year, moving-average series of the long-term interest rate. The focus here is to untangle the long-run relationship between bank risk exposure and the aggregate economic and financial variables.

In this study, the moving interest rate betas are not related to the macroeconomic and financial variables for two reasons. First, the interest rate risk for a financial institution is related to the maturity gap, or duration gap (see Akella and Greenbaum [1992]). The smaller the maturity gap is, the lower the interest rate beta will be. To run a meaningful regression on moving interest rate betas, the maturity gap has to be included as one of the regressors. Unfortunately, the time-series for the maturity gap for the commercial-banking industry is not available. Second, as reported below, the t-values for the estimated interest rate betas are small, on average, and insignificant most of the time.

SECTION 4.3
EMPIRICAL RESULTS

Estimated Market and Interest Rate Betas

Table 11 shows the summary statistics on the moving market betas, the moving interest rate betas, and the associated t-values. The Money-Center portfolio has the highest average and the highest standard deviation of the moving market betas (0.831 and 0.359, respectively). The Stable portfolio, as its name indicates, has the lowest standard deviation of the moving market

Table 11[a]

Summary statistics of the estimated market betas (MB) and the estimated interest rate betas (IB) using the moving regression technique, 1973-1990

Portfolio	Variable	Mean	Std. Dev.	Minimum	Maximum
Money-Center	MB	0.831	0.359	0.054	1.888
	IB	0.544	0.335	-0.291	1.374
	t_{MB}	4.292	1.788	0.384	8.569
	t_{IB}	1.622	1.009	-0.521	4.115
Stable	MB	0.653	0.175	0.415	1.230
	IB	0.258	0.154	-0.308	0.506
	t_{MB}	8.152	3.263	4.062	18.307
	t_{IB}	1.818	1.086	-0.997	4.556
All	MB	0.678	0.187	0.451	1.364
	IB	0.240	0.161	-0.348	0.498
	t_{MB}	8.466	3.015	3.986	15.346
	t_{IB}	1.729	1.180	-1.275	4.691
Moody's	MB	0.703	0.182	0.463	1.431
	IB	0.303	0.175	-0.322	0.589
	t_{MB}	8.005	2.981	3.680	14.880
	t_{IB}	1.966	1.217	-1.004	4.951

[a] The symbols t_{MB} and t_{IB} represent the t-ratios of the market and interest rate betas, respectively.

betas. Both the All and Moody's portfolio have summary statistics similar to those of the Stable portfolio. The estimated market betas for all four portfolios are significant at the 5% level; the minimum t-value is 1.984.

In contrast, the estimated interest rate betas range from negative and insignificant to positive and significant. The average t-values for the interest rate betas are much smaller than those for the market betas. These are consistent with the findings of Mitchell [1989] and Akella and Chen [1990], suggesting that, on the average, banks are quite efficient in hedging against interest rate volatility. For these reasons, the focus here is on explaining the market risks of commercial banks.

Results from the Second-Step Regression

Because the dependent variables and independent variables are moving average series, the error term in Equation 4.2.2 may be autocorrelated. Equation 4.2.2 is estimated by assuming that the error term is an autoregressive process of order 1. The regression results with an AR(1) correction are shown in Table 12. The robustness of the results in Table 12 are checked by running a linear regression with the robust-error options which assign a different order of lags of the autocorrelations.[6] The estimated coefficients, as well as their t-values, are very similar to the results reported in Table 12.

As shown in Table 12, the results for the Money-Center portfolio are different from those for the three other portfolios. The market beta for the Money-Center portfolio is not significantly related to both the short-term and the long-term interest rates; however, the market betas for the Stable, All, and Moody's portfolios are negatively related to the long-term interest rates (LRATE) and positively related to the short-term interest rates (SRATE). As the yield curve becomes flat or even inverted--due to an increase in the short-term interest rates, a decrease in the long-term interest rates, or both--the market risk of banks is likely to increase. These results suggest that the

Table 12
Regression results with AR(1) correction

The dependent variable is the estimated market beta using the moving regression technique, 1973-1990. There are 193 total observations. The t-values are in parentheses.

Variable	Money-Center	Stable	All	Moody's
Constant	-.1804	3.15**	3.60**	3.29*
	(-.05)	(2.16)	(2.27)	(1.65)
LRATE	-.0044	-.0969***	-.1136***	-.1063**
	(-.05)	(-2.73)	(-3.02)	(-2.32)
SRATE	-.0891	.0674***	.0737***	.0611*
	(-1.41)	(2.64)	(2.76)	(1.91)
M2	-.0007*	.0007***	.0006***	.0005**
	(-1.79)	(4.43)	(3.75)	(2.39)
IP	-.0489**	-.0440***	-.0509***	-.0520***
	(-2.10)	(-4.77)	(-5.12)	(-4.13)
ERATE	.0371***	.0041	.0087***	.0113***
	(5.79)	(1.59)	(3.17)	(3.35)
RLOAN	42.65***	7.80***	12.57***	15.34***
	(6.24)	(2.84)	(4.33)	(4.35)

Table 12 *(cont.)*

CLOAN	-15.27	-5.47	-8.38*	-9.01
	(-1.48)	(-1.34)	(-1.89)	(-1.62)
GSEC	-13.92*	-2.31	-4.87	-5.40
	(-1.66)	(-.69)	(-1.37)	(-1.24)
DW	2.049	2.236&	2.085	2.078
R^2	.965	.973	.978	.971
Adj. R^2	.963	.971	.977	.969

Notes: (1) *, **, and *** indicate significance at the 10%, 5%, and 1% levels, respectively (two-tailed test)

(2) & indicates that the Durbin-Watson (DW) test is inconclusive at the 5% level

market risks of the BHC's, with the exception of the money-center banks, are consistent with our expectations, i.e., the market risks of the money-center banks are less sensitive to interest rate changes. This may be due to the fact that money-center banks can hedge against the interest rate volatility better than smaller banks.

An expansionary monetary policy, indicated by an increase in M2, increases the market betas for all bank portfolios except the money-center banks. A loose monetary policy may enable banks to lend to risky businesses to which they normally would not be able. This may increase the default risks of bank loans and, hence, the market betas. The money-center banks, on the other hand, are not as sensitive as smaller banks to changes in monetary policy.[7]

A rise in the industrial production index (IP) decreases the market risk for all four portfolios. Hence, the market risks of BHC's tend to be lower when the economy is strong. Again, this is consistent with our expectations.

The strength of the U.S. dollar against major foreign currencies seems to increase the market risk of BHC's. This could be the result of either the higher default risk for bank international loan portfolios or the devaluation of foreign-currency holdings resulting from the U.S. dollar appreciation. In addition, the weighted exchange value of the U.S. dollar against major foreign currencies influences the risk of larger banks--especially money-center banks--more than that of smaller banks, as evidenced by the magnitude and t-values for the variable ERATE for each of the four portfolios. This is expected because larger banks--in particular money-center banks--tend to have larger international loan portfolios and foreign currency holdings.

Finally, the market risk of the BHC's is significantly positively related to the commercial real estate loan portfolio of the banking industry (RLOAN). This is consistent with the popular argument that increases in exposure to commercial real estate loans in the 1980's increased bank risk. The commercial and industrial loan ratio and the government securities ratio do not significantly affect the market risks of the four portfolios, which indicates that commercial and industrial loans and government securities are less risky than real estate loans. In sum, the results reported in Table 12 are consistent with the theoretical arguments outlined in Section 4.2.

Robustness of the Results

In addition to running linear regressions with robust-error options, the robustness of the results in Table 12 is examined by carrying out the following analysis. One issue raised in the time-series literature is the problem of potential nonstationarity of the variables used in a regression. A "spurious" relationship may result from the general trend in the time-series data. In such a case, Granger and Newbold [1974] suggest that the relationship should be estimated in the first difference of the variables (detrended) rather than in levels. However, running regressions in the first difference may bring about a loss of information concerning the long-run relationship of the variables--which is the major focus of this study. In spite of this, Equation 4.2.2 is run in first differences, and the results are reported in Table 13. The only significant change from Table 12 is that the long-term interest rate factor becomes insignificant in all regressions. The M2 is still significant at the 10% level for two of the portfolios, namely, the Stable and the All portfolios. The short-term interest rate factor, industrial production, and the real estate loan ratio still maintain their significance in Table 13. In general, the results from regressions with first differences are consistent with those in Table 12.

In addition to using two-year data (24 total observations) in order to estimate the moving market betas, three-, four-, and five-year data can be used to estimate the market betas. If more observations are used to estimate moving betas, two consequences arise: first, a reduction in the observations number and second, a reduction in variation. For example, if the three-

Table 13

OLS regression results

The dependent variable is the first difference of the estimated market beta using the moving regression technique, 1973-1990. The independent variables are first differences. There are 193 total observations. The t-values are in parentheses.

Variable	Money-Center	Stable	All	Moody's
Constant	-.0234	-.0106	-.0131	-.0086
	(-.87)	(-1.03)	(-1.22)	(-.71)
LRATE	.0264	-.0663	-.0657	-.0941
	(.17)	(-1.15)	(-1.09)	(-1.39)
SRATE	-.0489	.0600**	.0636**	.0541
	(-.62)	(1.97)	(2.00)	(1.51)
M2	.0013	.0014*	.0016*	.0011
	(.61)	(1.70)	(1.84)	(1.11)
IP	-.0724*	-.0501***	-.0604***	-.0541***
	(-1.83)	(-3.30)	(-3.80)	(-3.02)
ERATE	.0422***	.0058	.0097**	.0112**
	(4.09)	(1.46)	(2.36)	(2.39)

Table 13 *(cont.)*

RLOAN	46.04***	10.58**	15.21***	17.21***
	(3.55)	(2.13)	(2.92)	(2.93)
CLOAN	-27.83	-10.13	-14.08*	-10.17
	(-1.41)	(-1.34)	(-1.78)	(-1.14)
GSEC	-19.36	-4.65	-7.61	-5.87
	(-1.52)	(-.95)	(-1.48)	(-1.01)
DW	1.979	1.932	1.960	1.961
R^2	.108	.129	.125	.110
Adj. R^2	.065	.086	.082	.066

Note: *, **, and *** indicate significance at the 10%, 5%, and 1% levels, respectively (two-tailed test)

year (36 total observations) data are used, the estimated market betas are reduced from 193 to 181, and, more importantly, the standard deviation of the estimated market betas is also reduced. The reduction in variation is due to the smoothing effect from the moving regressions. When the second-step regression is run by using the market betas estimated from the three-year data, the results are similar to those reported in Table 12. However, the t-values for the estimated coefficients are reduced somewhat because of the reduced variation.

SECTION 4.4
SUMMARY AND CONCLUSION

This study seeks to answer the following two questions: first, *Have the market and interest rate risks that BHC's face changed in the last two decades and, if so, to what extent?*; and second, *If changes in the risks faced by BHC's have, in fact, occurred, can they be explained with macroeconomic variables and bank asset-composition variables?* These questions are answered using a two-step approach. In the first step, moving regressions are run with a two-index model (using market and interest rate indexes) for four stock portfolios of BHC's from 1973 to 1990. It was discovered that both the market and interest rate risks for banks varied substantially during the sample period. In the second step, the estimated market betas are regressed on a set of macroeconomic variables, including long-term and short-term interest rates, M2, industrial production, the exchange rate of the U.S. dollar against major foreign currencies, and three asset-composition indicators for the commercial-banking industry. Each of these macroeconomic variables and a bank's real estate loan exposure affect a bank's market risks. A positively-sloped yield curve and an expanding economy tend to contribute to the safety of the commercial-banking industry. Increases in the money supply tend to make banks riskier, and bank international exposure tends to increase their risk, as well, especially for money-center banks. Real estate loans, too, make banks riskier.

The macroeconomic and financial factors that are considered in this study are by no means exhaustive. However, the results in this book provide useful information for understanding the risks of commercial banks. In addition, the simple two-step approach developed here may be useful for bank regulators, managers, and other researchers in order to study the changing risk exposures of commercial banks due to other relevant economic factors.

Endnotes

1. One reason for the inconsistent conclusion about the interest rate risks is that different authors have used different measures of the interest rate factor and have examined different time periods. For detailed discussions, see Akella and Chen [1990] and Unal and Kane [1987].

2. The two-index model with market and interest rate factors can be motivated by Merton's [1973] Intertemporal Capital Asset Pricing Model (ICAPM). Details of the argument can be found in Chapter III.

3. For example, large banks may be more efficient in hedging risks; they tend to have more international loans and currency business.

4. Because of the considerable number of firms involved, a list of the 148 BHC's is not included in the Appendix. It will be made available upon request.

5. There is overlap across the four BHC groups.

6. The programs are run in RATS. In the linear regressions with robust-error options, the covariance matrix is estimated by using a procedure developed by Newey and West [1987], which has shown to yield a consistent, positive, semi-definite estimate of the covariance matrix in the presence of moving average and heteroskedastic residuals.

7. In a different context, Romer and Romer [1990] argue that the lending of large banks is less sensitive to changes in monetary policy. For example, in the case of an increase in the required reserve ratio, because large banks have access to other sources of funds, like large CD's, which are not subject to reserve requirements, their lending will not be affected by the stringent monetary policy.

APPENDICES

Appendix A. The NLSUR Estimation of Equation 2.2.1

Specifically, rewrite Equation 2.2.1 as,

$$\rho_j = r_i - \lambda_0 = \sum_{j=1}^{K} (\lambda_j \iota_T + f_j) b_{ij} + \epsilon_i, \quad i=1, ..., N$$

(A1.1)

where ι_T is a vector of T ones, and where the following Tx1 vectors are defined:

$$r_i = (r_i(1), ..., r_i(T))', \quad i=1, ..., N,$$
$$f_j = (f_j(1), ..., f_j(T))', \quad j=1, ..., K,$$
$$\epsilon_i = (\epsilon_i(1), ..., \epsilon_i(T))', \quad i=1, ..., N.$$
$$\lambda_0 = (\lambda_0(1), ..., \lambda_0(T))'.$$

The dependent variable in Equation A1.1 is the rate of excess return of the ith asset (the raw return minus the risk-free rate). Equation A1.1 can also be written as,

$$\rho_i = [(\lambda' \otimes \iota_T) + F] b_i + \epsilon_i$$
$$= X(\lambda) b_i + \epsilon_i, \quad i=1, ..., N,$$

where $\otimes$ denotes a Kronecker product and where,

$$\underset{Kx1}{\lambda} = (\lambda_1, ..., \lambda_K)',$$
$$\underset{TxK}{F} = (f_1, ..., f_K)',$$
$$\underset{Kx1}{b_i} = (b_{i1}, ..., b_{iK})', \quad i=1, ..., N.$$

Stacking the N equations gives,

$$\begin{bmatrix} \rho_1 \\ \rho_2 \\ \cdot \\ \cdot \\ \cdot \\ \rho_N \end{bmatrix} = \begin{bmatrix} X(\lambda) & 0 & ... & 0 & b_1 \\ 0 & X(\lambda) & ... & 0 & b_2 \\ \cdot & \cdot & \cdot & \cdot & \cdot \\ \cdot & \cdot & \cdot & \cdot & \cdot \\ \cdot & \cdot & \cdot & \cdot & \cdot \\ 0 & 0 & ... & X(\lambda) & b_N \end{bmatrix} + \begin{bmatrix} \epsilon_1 \\ \epsilon_2 \\ \cdot \\ \cdot \\ \cdot \\ \epsilon_N \end{bmatrix}$$

or, in notation,

$$\rho = [I_N \otimes X(\lambda)] b + \epsilon,$$

(A1.2)

and, with the assumption of the APT,

$$E(\epsilon) = 0_{NT}, \quad E(\epsilon\epsilon') = [\Sigma \otimes I_T].$$

We assume that the TxK factor matrix, F, as well as the NxK factor sensitivities matrix, $B = [b_{ij}]$, are of full-column rank. $T > N > K$ and $NT > K(N+1)$ are also assumed to ensure that Equation A1.2 has more equations than unknowns. Given these assumptions, the necessary condition in order for the NLSUR estimators to exist is satisfied: the Jacobian of the response function in (7),

$$J (\lambda', b') = \frac{\partial}{\partial (\lambda', b')} ([I_N \otimes X (\lambda)] b) =$$

$$[B \otimes \iota, I_N \; 0 \; X (\lambda)] , \qquad (A1.3)$$

is of full-column rank.

NLSUR estimators may be obtained in three steps. Step (i) is to estimate Equation A1.1 via an equation-by-equation (i.e., asset-by-asset) OLS. The residuals, $\hat{e}_i$'s, are then used to estimate Σ as $\hat{\Sigma} = [\hat{\sigma}_{ij}] = [T^{-1} \hat{e}_i \; ' \; \hat{e}_j]$ in Step (ii). In Step (iii), the NLSUR estimator, $(\tilde{\lambda}, \tilde{b})$ is chosen to minimize the quadratic form,

$$Q (\lambda, b; \hat{\Sigma}) = (\rho - [I_N \otimes X (\lambda)] b)' \; (\hat{\Sigma}^{-1} \otimes I_T)$$

$$(\rho - [I_N \otimes X (\lambda)] b) \qquad (A1.4)$$

With the additional regularity conditions given by Gallant [1975, 1987], $(\tilde{\lambda}', \tilde{b}')$ is strongly consistent for (λ', b'), and $T^{1/2} [(\tilde{\lambda}, \tilde{b}') - (\lambda', b')]$ is asymptotically normal with mean zero and covariance matrix Ω^{-1} for which $\tilde{\Omega}^{-1}$ is a strongly consistent estimator where,

$$\tilde{\Omega} = T^{-1} J' (\tilde{\lambda}', \tilde{b}') (\tilde{\Sigma}^{-1} \; 0 \; I_T) J (\tilde{\lambda}', \tilde{b}') , \qquad (A1.5)$$

where $J(\tilde{\lambda}', \tilde{b}')$ denotes $J(.)$ evaluated at $(\tilde{\lambda}', \tilde{b}')$.

Appendix B. The Real Interest Rate Model

Fama and Gibbons [1984] follow the work of Irving Fisher [1930] and break the one-month interest rate, TB_{t-1}--observed at the end of month t-1--into an expected real return for month t, ER_{t-1}, and an expected inflation rate, EI_{t-1},

$$TB_{t-1} = ER_{t-1} + EI_{t-1} . \tag{A2.1}$$

The works of Hess and Bichsler [1975], Fama [1976], Grabade and Wachtel [1978], and Fama and Gibbons [1982] suggest a model in which the expected real return is a random walk. The ex-post real return for month t can be expressed as,

$$TB_{t-1} - I_t = ER_{t-1} + \xi_t , \tag{A2.2}$$

and then the difference between the real returns for t and t-1 is,

$$(TB_{t-1} - I_t) - (Tb_{t-2} - I_{t-1}) = \Delta ER_{t-1} + \xi_t - \xi_{t-1} , \tag{A2.3}$$

where ΔER_{t-1} is the change in the expected real return from month t-1 to month t, and ξ_t is the unexpected component of the real return for month t. If ER_{t-1} is a random walk, ΔER_{t-1} and ξ_t are both white noise. The difference between the real returns for months t and t-1 can be represented as a first-order moving average process (see Box and Jenkins [1976], Ch. 4),

$$(TB_{t-1} - I_t) - (TB_{t-2} - I_{t-1}) = u_t - \Theta u_{t-1} , \tag{A2.4}$$

and the moving average parameter, Θ, is close to 1.0 (0.0) when the variance of ξ_t is large (small) relative to the variance of ΔER_{t-1}.

Nonlinear least squares is used to estimate the moving average parameter, Θ; the monthly data for June, 1976-December, 1987 yield,

$$(TB_{t-1} - I_t) - (TB_{t-2} - I_{t-1}) = u_t - 0.4282\, u_{t-1} . \tag{A2.5}$$
$$(0.022)$$

The estimated expected real return for month t implied by Equation A2.4 is the fitted value,

$$ER_{t-1} = (TB_{t-2} - I_{t-1}) - 0.4282\, u_{t-1} . \tag{A2.6}$$
$$(0.022)$$

The real return for month t-1 is expressed as,

$$TB_{t-2} - I_{t-1} = ER_{t-2} + u_{t-1} . \tag{A2.7}$$

Equation A2.6 then becomes,

$$ER_{t-1} = ER_{t-2} + (1-0.4282)\, u_{t-1} . \tag{A2.8}$$

Using the expected real return estimated from Equation A2.8, the expected inflation rate for month t extracted from the one-month treasury bill rate is,

$$EITB_{t-1} = TB_{t-1} - ER_{t-1} .$$

The unexpected inflation rate is $UI_t = I_t - EITB_{t-1}$.

Appendix C. An Interpretation of the Factor Risk Premium, λ_j

One way to interpret the λ_j in Equation 2.1.3 is to specialize the APT to an explicit stochastic environment within which individual equilibrium is achieved. Cox, Ingersoll and Ross' [1985] (CIR) intertemporal diffusion model provides a convenient framework for this purpose. Suppose that there are k exogenous, independent (without loss of generality) factors, s^j, which follow a multivariate diffusion process and whose current values are sufficient statistics to determine the current state of the economy. As a consequence, the current price, p_i, of each asset i will be a function only of $s = (s^1, ..., s^k)$ and the particular fixed contractual conditions which define that asset in the next differential time unit. The random return, dr_i, on asset i will depend on the random movements of the factors. By the diffusion assumption we can write,

$$dr_i = E_i \, dt + b_{i1} \, ds^1 + ... + b_{ik} \, ds^k .$$

It follows that the conditions of the APT are satisfied exactly with $d\epsilon_i = 0$, and the APT pricing relationship (2.1.3) must hold exactly under no arbitrage assumption.

If individuals in this economy are solving consumption withdrawal problems, then the current utility of future consumption--e.g., the discounted expected value of the utility of future consumption, v--will be a function only of the individual's current wealth, w, and the current state of nature, s. The individual will optimize by choosing a consumption withdrawal plan, c, and an optimal portfolio choice, x, so as to maximize the expected increment in v, i.e.,

$$\underset{x,c}{\text{Max}} \; E(dv) .$$

At an optimum, consumption will be withdrawn to the point where its marginal utility equals the marginal utility of wealth,

$$u'(c) = V_u .$$

The individual portfolio choice will result from the optimization of a locally quadratic form, exactly as the static CAPM theory with the additional feature that covariances of the change in wealth, dw, along with the changes in state variables,

ds^i, will now be influenced by portfolio choice and will, in general, alter the optimal portfolio. By solving this optimization problem and using the marginal utility condition, $u'(c) = V_m$, the individual equilibrium sets factor risk premia equal to,

$$E^j - E_0 = (R/C) \, (\partial c / \partial s^j) \, \sigma_j^2 \, ,$$

where $R = -(wV_{ww})/V_w$ is the individual coefficient of relative risk aversion and σ_j^2 is the local variance of factor s_j. The premia, $E^j - E_0$ can be negative if consumption moves counter to the state variable.

One special case is when the utility function is log case, $R = 1$; then,

$$E^j - E_0 = (\Sigma_i \, x_i \, b_{ij}) \, \sigma_j^2 \, ,$$

where x is the individual optimal portfolio. This form emphasizes the general relationship between b_j and σ_j^2. Normalizing $\Sigma_i \, x_i \, b_{ij}$ to unity by scaling s^j, we have,

$$E^j - E_0 = \sigma_j^2 \, .$$

The risk premium of factor j is its variance.

For other utility functions, individual consumption vectors can be expressed in terms of portfolios of returns, and similar expressions can be obtained,

$$E^j - E_0 = [\Sigma_i \, w_1 \, R_1 \, (1/c_1) \, (\partial c_1 / \partial s_j)] \sigma_j^2 \, ,$$

where 1 represents the 1th investor and R_1 is her relative risk-aversion coefficient; w_1 is the proportion of total wealth held by investor 1; $(1/c_1) \, (\partial c_1 / \partial s_j)$ is the partial elasticity of her consumption with respect to changes in the jth factor; and σ_j^2 is the variance of the jth factor. In general, the greater the variance of the factor, the greater the risk premia.

Appendix D. Estimates of the Two-Factor Model with Macroeconomic Variables as the Condition Set

In Equations 3.2.5-3.2.11, means, covariances, and variances can be conditioned on macroeconomic variables. The four macroeconomic variables from Song [1990]--the difference in the return of a long-term government bond and a one-month treasury bill, industrial production, the default risk premia, and unexpected inflation--are chosen since they are shown to be relevant for deposit-institution stock returns. AR(1) for each mean, covariance, and variance is specified. The model is,

$$r_i(t) = \frac{\alpha_0^i + \sum_{j=1}^{4} \alpha_j^i E_j(t-1)}{\gamma_0 + \sum_{j=1}^{4} \gamma_j E_j(t-1)} E(f_1(t)) + \frac{\beta_0^i + \sum_{j=1}^{4} \beta_j^i E_j(t-1)}{1_0 + \sum_{j=1}^{4} 1_j E_j(t-1)} E(f_2(t)),$$

$$i = 1, 2, 3$$

$$f_1(t) = E(f_1(t)) + \epsilon_t = \alpha_0 + \sum_{j=1}^{4} \alpha_j E_j(t-1) + \epsilon_t,$$

$$f_2(t) = E(f_2(t)) + \omega_t = \beta_0 + \sum_{j=1}^{4} \beta_j E_j(t-1) + \omega_t,$$

$$\epsilon_t u_t^i = \alpha_0 + \sum_{j=1}^{4} \alpha_j^i E_j(t-1) + f_t^i, \qquad i = 1, 2, 3,$$

$$\omega_t u_t^i = \beta_0^i + \sum_{j=1}^{4} \beta_j^i E_j(t-1) + \delta_t,$$

$$\epsilon_t^2 = \gamma_0 + \sum_{j=1}^{4} \gamma_j E_j(t-1) + v_t,$$

$$\omega_t^2 = 1_0 + \sum_{j=1}^{4} 1_j E_j(t-1) + z_t,$$

where E_j, $j = 1, 4$, are the four macroeconomic variables; other notations are the same as in Table 7.

Table 14

Estimates of the two-factor model with macroeconomic variables as the condition set

α_0	α_1	α_2	α_3	α_4		β_0	β_1	β_2	β_3	β_4
-0.00	1.55	-0.28	0.77	-0.51		0.02*	-0.85	-0.78*	-3.14*	0.98*
(0.10)	(1.53)	(0.58)	(0.51)	(1.50)		(2.91)	(1.15)	(2.18)	(2.84)	(3.95)
γ_0	γ_1	γ_2	γ_3	γ_4		l_0	l_1	l_2	l_3	l_4
0.01	0.04	0.01	0.06	0.00		0.09	0.04	0.01*	0.06	0.02
(1.72)	(0.43)	(0.32)	(0.39)	(0.01)		(3.10)	(0.40)	(3.38)	(0.09)	(0.87)

Deposit-Institution Stock Portfolios

	RP_1^1	RP_2^2	RP_3^3
	α_0^1	α_0^2	α_0^3
	0.01*	0.00	0.03*
	(2.07)	(1.58)	(2.03)
	α_1^1	α_1^2	α_1^3
	-0.04	-0.02	-0.02
	(0.32)	(0.15)	(0.24)
	α_2^1	α_2^2	α_2^3
	-0.01	-0.06	-0.01
	(0.15)	(0.79)	(0.11)

Table 14 (cont.)

Deposit-Institution Stock Portfolios

RP^1_1		RP^2_2		RP^3_3	
α^1_3	-0.06	α^2_3	0.02	α^3_3	0.01
	(0.33)		(0.11)		(0.05)
α^1_4	0.02	α^2_4	-0.02	α^3_4	0.04
	(0.45)		(0.48)		(1.05)
β^1_0	0.01	β^2_0	0.03*	β^3_0	0.01*
	(1.59)		(2.58)		(2.63)
β^1_1	-0.04	β^2_1	-0.02	β^3_1	-0.06
	(0.68)		(0.15)		(1.16)
β^1_2	-0.07*	β^2_2	-0.06	β^3_2	-0.06*
	(2.37)		(0.79)		(2.81)
β^1_3	-0.05	β^2_3	0.03	β^3_3	-0.03
	(0.55)		(0.11)		(0.44)

Table 14 (cont.)

<u>Deposit-Institution Stock Portfolios</u>

β_4^1	β_4^2	β_4^3
0.01	-0.02	0.02
(0.67)	(0.48)	(0.91)

Test of Overidentifying Restrictions
$\chi^2 (12) = 21.03$
p-value = 0.05

Appendix E.   Sample Bank Holding Companies

Bank Holding Company	Exchange Code

1. Money-Center Portfolio (9)

BankAmerica Corp.	N
Bankers Trust NY Corp.	N
Chase Manhattan Corp.	N
Chemical Banking Corp.	N
Citicorp	N
Continental Bank Corp.	N
First Chicago Corp.	N
Manufacturers Hanover Corp.	N
Morgan J.P. & Co., Inc.	N

2. Stable Portfolio (68)

Affiliated Bankshares Colo., Inc.	O
Ameritrust Corp.	O
Banco Popular DE, P.R.	O
Bancoklahoma Corp.	O
Bancorp Hawaii, Inc.	O
Bank New York, Inc.	N
Bank of Boston Corp.	N
Bank South Corp.	O
Banks Iowa, Inc.	O
Banks Mid America, Inc.	O
Banponce Corp.	O
Baybanks, Inc.	O
Boatmens Bancshares, Inc.	O
Central Bancshares South, Inc.	O
Central Fidelity Banks, Inc.	O
Colorado National Bankshares, Inc.	O
Comerica, Inc.	O
Commerce Bancshares, Inc.	O

Corestates Financial Corp.	O
Crestar Financial Corp.	O
Deposit Guaranty Corp.	O
Dominion Bankshares Corp.	O
Equimark Corp.	N
First Alabama Bancshares, Inc.	O
First American Corp., TN	O
First Commerce Corp., New Orleans	O
First Fidelity Bancorporation, NE	N
First Florida Banks, Inc.	O
First Hawaiian, Inc.	O
First Interstate Bancorp	N
First Security Corp., DE	O
First Tennessee National Corp.	O
First Virginia Banks, Inc.	N
Firstar Corp. New	N
Fleet Norstar Financial Group	N
Fourth Financial Corp.	O
Huntington Bankshares, Inc.	O
INB Financial Corp.	O
Manufacturers National Corp.	O
Marshall & Ilsley Corp.	O
Mercantile Bancorporation, Inc.	O
Mercantile Bankshares Corp.	O
Meridian Bancorp, Inc.	O
Michigan National Corp.	O
Midlantic Corp.	O
Northeast Bancorp, Inc.	O
Northern Trust Corp.	O
Norwest Corp.	N
Republic New York Corp.	N
Riggs National Corp., Washington, D.C.	O
Signet Banking Corp.	N
Society Corp.	O
South Carolina National Corp.	O
Southeast Banking Corp.	N

Southtrust Corp.	O
Star Banc Corp.	O
State Street Boston Corp.	O
Sterling Bancorp	N
Trustmark Corp.	O
UJB Financial Corp.	N
United Banks Colorado, Inc.	O
United Missouri Bancshares, Inc.	O
United States Bancorp, OR	O
United States Trust Corp.	O
Valley National Corp., AZ	O
Wells Fargo & Co. New	N
Wilmington Trust Co., DE	O
Zions Bancorp	O

3. All Portfolio (148)

   (Omitted)

4. Moody's Portfolio (100)

   (Omitted; see Moody's 1991 Banking and Finance Manual)

Note: N and O are the exchange codes for the NYSE/AMEX and NASDAQ, respectively.

References

Abell, J.D. and Krueger, T.M., Macroeconomic Influences on Beta, *Journal of Economics and Business*, 41(2): 185-190, May, 1989.

Aharony, Joseph, Sauders, Anthony and Swary, Itzhek, The Effects of Shift in Monetary Policy Regime on the Profitability and Risk of Commercial Banks, *Journal of Monetary Economics*, Vol. 17, 363-377, 1986.

Akella, S.R. and Chen, S.J., Interest Rate Sensitivity of Bank Stock Returns: Specification Effects and Structural Changes *Journal of Financial Research*, 13(2): 147-154, Summer 1990.

Akella, S.R. and Greenbaum, S.I., Innovations in Interest Rates, Duration Transformation, and Bank Stock Returns, *Journal of Money, Credit, and Banking*, 24: 27-42, February, 1992.

Bae, Sung C., Interest Rate Changes and Common Stock Returns of Financial Institutions: Revisited, *Journal of Financial Research* 13(1): 71-79, Spring 1990.

Barsky, Robert B., Why Don't the Prices of Stocks and Bonds Move Together?, *American Economic Review*, Vol. 79, No. 5, December, 1989.

Benston, G.J., Eisenbeis, R.A., Horvitz, P.M., Kane, E.J. and Kaufman, G.G., *Perspectives on Safe & Sound Banking, Past, Present, and Future*, MIT Press, 1986.

Bodurtha, James and Mark, Nelson C., Testing the CAPM with Time-Varying Risks and Returns, *Journal of Finance*, Vol. 46, No. 4, pp. 1485-1505, September, 1991.

Bollerslev, T., Chou, R.Y., Jayaraman, N. and Kroner, K.F., ARCH Modeling in Finance: A Selective Review of the Theory and Empirical Evidence, With Suggestions for Future Research, Manuscript, Northwestern University, 1990.

Booth, J.R. and Officer, D.T., Expectations, Interest Rates, and Commercial Bank Stocks, *Journal of Financial Research*, Spring 1985, 51-58.

Booth, J.R., Officer, D.T. and Henderson, G.V., Commercial Bank Stocks, Interest Rates, and Systematic Risk, *Journal of Economics and Business*, 37(4): 303-310, December, 1985.

Box, G.E.P. and Jenkins, G.M., *Time Series Analysis: Forecasting and Control*, Holden-Day, San Francisco, CA, 1976.

Breeden, Douglas T., An Intertemporal Asset Pricing Models with Stochastic Investment Opportunities, *Journal of Financial Economics*, Vol. 7, No. 3, pp. 711-743, June, 1983.

Brewer, Elijah III and Lee, Cheng F., The Impact of Market, Industry, and Interest Rate Risks on Bank Stock Returns, Federal Reserve Bank of Chicago Staff Memo, 1985.

Brown, S.J. and Weinstein, M.I., A New Approach to Testing Asset Pricing Models: The Bilinear Paradigm, *Journal of Finance*, 38, pp. 711-743, 1983.

Chamberlain, G. and Rothschild, M., Arbitrage, Factor Structure, and Mean-Variance Analysis on Large Asset Markets, *Econometrica*, 51, 1281-1304, September, 1983.

Chamberlain, Gary, Funds, Factors, and Diversification in Arbitrage Pricing Models, *Econometrica*, 51, 1305-1323, 1983.

Chan, K.C., Chen, N.F. and Hsieh, D.A., An Exploratory Investigation of the Firm Size Effect, *Journal of Financial Economics*, 1985, 451-471.

Chance, Don M. and Lane, William R., A Re-examination of Interest Rate Sensitivity in the Common Stocks of Financial Institutions, *Journal of Financial Research*, Vol. 3, 1983.

Chen, Nai-fu, Some Empirical Tests of the Theory of Arbitrage Pricing, *Journal of Finance*, Vol. 38, pp. 1392-1414, December, 1983.

Chen, Nai-fu, Roll, Richard and Ross, S.A., Economic Forces and the Stock Market, *Journal of Business*, Vol. 59, No. 3, 1986.

Cho, D.C., Elton, Edwin J. and Gruber, Martin J., On the Robustness of the Roll and Ross APT Methodology, *Journal of Financial and Quantitative Analysis*, Vol. 19, pp. 1-10, March, 1984.

Choi, J.J., Elyasiani E. and Kopechy, K.J., The Sensitivity of Bank Stock Returns to Market, Interest and Exchange Rate Risks, *Journal of Banking and Finance*, 16: 983-1004, 1992.

Cox, John C., Ingersoll, Jonathan E. Jr. and Ross, Stephen A., An Intertemporal General Equilibrium Model of Asset Prices, *Econometrica*, Vol. 53, No. 3, pp. 363-384, March, 1985.

Dhrymes, Phoebus, Friend, Irwin and Gultekin, B., A Critical Examination of the Empirical Evidence on the Arbitrage Pricing Theory, *Journal of Finance*, Vol. 39, No. 2, pp. 323-346, June, 1984.

Engle, Robert F., Autoregressive Conditional Heteroskedasticity with Estimates of the Variances of United Kingdom Inflation, *Econometrica*, 50, 987-1007, 1982.

Fama, Eugene F., *Foundations of Finance*, New York: Basic Books, 1976.

------, Inflation Uncertainty and Expected Returns on Treasury Bills, *Journal of Political Economy*, 84, 427-448.

Fama, Eugene F. and Gibbons, Michael R., Risk, Return, and Equilibrium: Empirical Tests, *Journal of Monetary Economics*, 13(1984): 327-348, North-Holland.

Flannery, Mark J. and James, Christopher M., The Effect of Interest Rate Changes on the Common Stock Returns of Financial Institutions, *Journal of Finance*, Vol. 39, September, 1984.

Gallant, A. Ronald., Seemingly Unrelated Nonlinear Regressions, *Journal of Econometrics*, Vol. 3, No. 1, pp. 35-50, February, 1975.

------, *Nonlinear Statistical Models*, New York: John Wiley and Sons, Inc., 1987.

Gallant, A.R. and Jorgenson, D.W., Statistical Inference for a System Simultaneous, Nonlinear, Implicit Equations, *Journal of Econometrics*, 11, 275-302, 1979.

Garbade, Kenneth and Wachtel, Daul, Time Variation in the Relationship Between Inflation and Interest Rates, *Journal of Monetary Economics*, 4, 755-765, 1978.

Giliberto, Mark, Interest Rate Sensitivity in the Common Stocks of Financial Intermediaries: A Methodological Note, *Journal of Financial and Quantitative Analysis* 20(1): 123-126, March, 1985.

Giliberto, Mark and Titman, Sheridan, The Relation Between Mean-Variance Efficiency and Arbitrage Pricing, *Journal of Business*, 60, 97-112, 1987.

Granger, C.W.J. and Newbold, P., Spurious Regressions in Econometrics, *Journal of Econometrics*, 2:111-120, 1974.

Grinblatt, Mark and Titman, Sheridan, Factor Pricing in a Finite Economy, *Journal of Financial Economics*, Vol. 12, pp. 497-507, December, 1983.

------, Approximate Factor Structures: Interpretations and Implications for Empirical Tests, *Journal of Finance*, Vol. 40, No. 5, pp. 1367-1373, September, 1985.

Hansen, Lars P., Large Sample Properties of Generalized Method Moments Estimators, *Econometrica*, 50, 1029-1054, 1982.

Hardouvelis, G.A., Macroeconomic Information and Stock Prices, *Journal of Economics and Business*, 39:131-140, 1987.

Harvey, Campbell, Time-Varying Conditional Covariances in Tests of Asset Pricing Models, Working paper, Fuqua School of Business, Duke University, 1988.

Hess, Patrick J. and Bicksler, James L., Capital Asset Prices versus Time Series Models as Predictors of Inflation: The Expected Real Interest and Market Efficiency, *Journal of Financial Economics* 2, 341-360, 1975.

Huberman, Gar, A Simple Approach to Arbitrage Pricing Theory, *Journal of Economic Theory*, Vol. 28, pp. 183-191, 1982.

Huberman, Gar, Kandel, Shumuel and Stambaugh, Robert F., Mimicking Portfolios and Exact Arbitrage Pricing, *Journal of Finance*, 42, 1-9, 1987.

Ibbotson Associates, *Stocks, Bonds, Bills, and Inflation: 1988 Year Book*, Chicago, 1988.

------, *Stocks, Bonds, Bills, and Inflation: 1991 Year Book*, Chicago, 1991.

Ingersoll, Jonathan E. Jr., *Theory of Financial Decision Making*, Rowman & Littlefield, 1987.

Kandel, Shmuel and Stambaugh, Robert F., On Correlations and Inferences about Mean-Variance Efficiency, *Journal of Financial Economics*, 18, 61-90, 1987.

Kane, Edward J. and Unal, Haluk, Change in Market Assessment of Deposit-Institution Riskiness, *Journal of Financial Service Research*, 1:201-229, 1988.

Kim, M.K. and Wu, C., Macro-economic Factors and Stock Returns, *Journal of Financial Research*, 10(2): 87-98, 1987.

Kwan, Simon H., Re-examination of Interest Rate Sensitivity of Commercial Bank Stock Returns Using a Random Coefficient Model, *Journal of Financial Services Research*, 5:61-76, 1991.

Lehmann, Bruce and Modest, David, The Empirical Foundations of the Arbitrage Pricing Theory, *Journal of Financial Economics*, 21, 213-254, 1988.

Lloyd, William P. and Shick, Richard A., A Test of Stone's Two-Index Model of Returns, *Journal of Financial and Quantitative Analysis*, Vol. 12, 363-376, September, 1977.

Long, John B., Stock Prices, Inflation, and the Term Structure of Interest Rates, *Journal of Financial Economics*, Vol. 1, pp. 131-170, 1974.

Lynge, Morgan J. and Kenton, Zumwalt J., An Empirical Study of the Interest Rate Sensitivity of Commercial Bank Returns: A Multi-Index Approach, *Journal of Financial and Quantitative Analysis*, Vol. 15, 731-742, September, 1980.

Mark, N.C., Time-Varying Betas and Risk Premia in the Pricing of Forward and Foreign Exchange Contracts, *Journal of Financial Economics*, Vol. 22, pp. 335-354, 1988.

McElroy, Marjorie B., Burmeister, Edwin and Wall, Kent D., Two Estimators for the APT Model When Factors are Measured, *Economic Letters*, Vol. A, No. 3, pp. 271-275, 1985.

McElroy, Marjorie B. and Burmeister, Edwin, Arbitrage Pricing Theory as a Restricted Nonlinear Multivariate Regression Model: ITNLSUR ESTIMATES, *Journal of Business and Economic Statistics*, January, 1988.

Merton, Robert C., An Intertemporal Capital Asset Pricing Model, *Econometrica*, Vol. 41, pp. 867-888, September, 1973.

Mitchell, K., Interest Rate Risk at Commercial Banks: An Empirical Investigation, *The Financial Review*, 24(3): 431-455, August, 1989.

Newey, W. and West, K., A Simple, Positive Semi-definite, Heteroskedasticity and Autocorrelation Consistent Covariance Matrix, *Econometrica*, 55(3): 703-708, May, 1987.

Peltzman, Sam., Toward a More General Theory of Regulation, *Journal of Economics*, 19, 211-241, 1976.

Pettway, Richard H. and Jordan, Bradford D., APT vs. CAPM Estimates of the Return-generating Function Parameters for Regulated Public Utilities, *Journal of Financial Research*, Vol. X, No. 3, Fall 1987.

Roll, Richard and Ross, Stephen A., An Empirical Investigation of the Arbitrage Pricing Theory, *Journal of Finance*, Vol. 35, No. 5, pp. 1073-1103, December, 1980.

Romer, C. and Romer, D., New Evidence on the Monetary Transmission Mechanism, *Brookings Papers on Economic Activities*, 1, 1990.

Rosenberg, Bar and Perry, Philip R., The Fundamental Determinants of Risk in Banking, in "*Risk and Capital Adequacy in Commercial Banks,*" ed. by Sherman J. Maisel, The University of Chicago Press, 1981.

Ross, Stephen A., The Arbitrage Theory of Capital Asset Pricing, *Journal of Economic Theory*, Vol. 13, No. 3, 341-360, 1976.

------, Return, Risk and Arbitrage, in Irwin Friend and James Bickler (eds.), *Risk and Return in Finance*, Vol. 1, Cambridge, MA: Ballinger, 1977.

Scholes M., The Relationship Between the Returns on Bonds and the Returns on Common Stocks, Mimeograph, Massachusetts Institute of Technology, November, 1971.

Scott, William L. and Peterson, Richard L., Interest Rate Risk and Equity Values of Hedged and Unhedged Financial Intermediaries, *Journal of Financial Research*, Vol. 9, pp. 325-329, 1986.

Shanken, Jay, Intertemporal Asset Pricing: An Empirical Investigation, *Journal of Econometrics*, July-August, 1990, 45(1-2), pp. 99-120.

Sharpe, William F., The Capital Asset Pricing Model: A 'Multi-Beta' Interpretation, in *Financial Decision Making Under Uncertainty*, Haim Levy and Marshall Sarrat eds., New York: Academic Press, 1977.

Sinkey, Joseph F., *Commercial Bank Management*, 2nd ed., New York: Macmillan Publishing Co., 1986.

Song, Frank M., The Macroeconomic Risks of Deposit Institutions, Manuscript, Ohio State University, 1990.

------, A Two-Factor ARCH Model For Deposit-Institution Stock Returns, forthcoming, *Journal of Money, Credit, and Banking*.

Stone, B.K., Systematic Interest Rate Risk in a Two-index Model of Returns, *Journal of Financial and Quantitative Analysis*, 9:709-721, November, 1974.

Sweeney, Richard J. and Warga, Arthur D., The Pricing of Interest-Rate: Evidence from the Stock Market, *Journal of Finance*, Vol. 41, pp. 393-410, 1986.

Thistle, P.D., Mcleod, R.W. and Conrad, B.L., Interest Rates and Bank Portfolio Adjustments, *Journal of Banking and Finance*, 13:151-161, 1989.

Unal, Haluk and Kane, E.J., Off-Balance-Sheet Items and the Changing Market Sensitivity of Deposit-Institution Equity Returns, Proceedings of Federal Reserve Bank of Chicago Conference on Bank Structure and Competition, pp. 432-455, 1987.

Yourougou, Pierre, Interest-Rate and the Pricing of Depository Financial Intermediary Common Stock, Empirical Evidence, *Journal of Banking and Finance*, 14(1990), 803-820.